Feedback via social media?
Client service via social media

Increase tech IQ

HR increase tech IQ. Royalty/Retention

BUILDING DRAGONS

DIGITAL TRANSFORMATION IN THE EXPERIENCE ECONOMY

DANIEL NEWMAN WITH OLIVIER BLANCHARD

whats after
SHIELD and EWV?
. User experience?

Be First in a
category.

BUILDING DRAGONS

Daniel Newman with Olivier Blanchard

ISBN-13: 978-0692696354 (Broadsuite, Inc.)
ISBN-10: 0692696350

First Printing 2016

Publisher
Broadsuite, Inc.
T: 817-480-3038
www.broadsuite.com

TABLE OF CONTENTS

INTRODUCTION:

CHASING UNICORNS VS. BUILDING DRAGONS

As the business world becomes increasingly rooted in new technologies, innovation and disruption, it is interesting (even ironic) to note that the vocabulary we use to identify new and emerging business mechanisms connects us so much to our mythological past. Read any article about the intersection of technology and business these days and you will invariably bump into mentions of *unicorns*, wizards, the *holy grail* of this and that, phoenixes, *enchanted* objects, and even *dragons* (not to mention entire armies of trolls).

Among the seemingly endless mythological references to be found in business and tech discussions in recent years, no creature has come to be more revered than the unicorn. A unicorn is a company, usually a startup, that scales user adoption so fast that it reaches a billion dollar valuation before it even has a proven business plan. In many ways, the unicorn has come to embody the spirit of Silicon Valley. It has become a vessel for every entrepreneur's dream of statistically improbable success against impossible odds in the most competitive entrepreneurial environment in the world, no less. If there is a broader American Dream of "making it big" in Hollywood or sports or music, building a unicorn — or investing in one — is the Silicon Valley version of it.

Every entrepreneurial high school and college student developing an application wants to build the next great company — the next Apple, Facebook, Google, or Youtube — and the most direct path to that kind of success seems to be building a unicorn (or *unicorns*, plural, as that particular journey tends to reward a bend toward trial and error *and* serial entrepreneurship).

The odds of making that dream come true, though, are millions to one. Even if you have the best idea in the world, at the right moment, and with the right resources and the right plan, you still have to get lucky and then *keep* getting lucky long enough to scale. You have to keep scoring wins as your product matures and evolve. You also have to repeatedly reinvent your product(s) to keep disrupting your industry before it either disrupts you or moves on to the next hot new startup or fad.

In the past, that kind of against-all-odds success has tended to give birth to *legendary* companies like Disney, Nike, Amazon, Sony, and perhaps even Tesla (time will tell). Even if you aren't familiar with Jungian archetypes, you naturally notice something familiar about these brands. Their stories read like heroes' journeys — modest beginnings, heroic insurgencies against powerful but lumbering incumbents, and long, successful reigns once they finally take their place on their respective thrones. Their stories are, like all enduring tales, rooted in popular myths, which is probably why we subconsciously feel the need to wrap them in magical nomenclatures. After all, what is mythology if not a lens through which to understand the world around us? As it turns out, the intersection of business and tech is no different in that regard.

There's a catch, though. As the rarest, most beloved of all mythical creatures, the unicorn also should be the most powerful, but that isn't the case. In the world of business, a unicorn is a company that doesn't have an established success or performance record yet. In this context, a unicorn's valuation is based on what it *might* have the power to do, rather than what it *can* do. In terms of success and payouts, the legend of the unicorn is different from the statistical reality of the unicorn.

Seen through that lens, the term "unicorn" might seem more cynical than aspirational. It implies a certain degree of skepticism, even scorn. In this context, believing in unicorns is a little like rounding up a bunch of errant, promising young colts and hoping that, while you nurture them in your stable, one of them will magically grown a horn in the middle of its forehead. Even the nurturing model itself can sometimes seem more like alchemy than any kind of legitimate process. (Just throwing money at something doesn't guarantee its long-term success.) In short, the term "unicorn" pitches *potential* against *execution*. While it refers to companies working on some of the world's most innovative and disruptive ideas — ideas with tremendous potential for change, good, forward momentum, and for *real* and tangible success — in their current state, they have little idea how to deliver on any of it, let alone exist in any sustainable way beyond the user adoption phase. Why? Because, in their magical world, scale builds rainbows, and the mythical pot of gold waiting for them at the end of each one is called an IPO. Unicorns aren't necessarily built to last. Most are built for a different kind of financial game.

In the business world, the unicorn is, more often than not, a mirage, an unrealized idea, fragile and ephemeral. Its fatal flaw is that, until it reaches maturity (assuming it ever does), it cannot sustain itself. It doesn't know how, and as long as investors stick around, it doesn't need to. In other words, the unicorn lacks the continuous profit driving capability that real businesses need to innovate, grow and thrive, especially in competitive business environments.

In light of this, the business question becomes: If not unicorns, what? What should be the model? What other mythical business beast should investors and executives look for and apply resources to? Can the unicorn's potential for transformative innovation somehow be combined with the drive and experience to execute on it? Does this combination of traits exist in one creature? The answer that comes to mind for those of us who have been keeping an eye on every promising business model is yes. They're called dragons. (Don't laugh. Dragons are actually a thing.)

So... what is a dragon, exactly? It depends who you ask. In the VC world, a dragon tends to be any startup that returns (pays out) an entire fund (which makes it far rarer and more valuable than a unicorn). For everyone else in the business world, a dragon isn't necessarily a startup. Dragons are established or maturing businesses that rely on their original start-up mindsets to *adapt* to and *disrupt* markets them as a means of dominating them. Dragons are everything unicorns aren't— alert, adaptive, innovative, agile, sustainable, profit-driven, resilient, and wise.

Dragons typically come in one of two forms. The first is the *changeling dragon*, which innovates its way to adaptation and change but doesn't usually give birth to other dragons. Examples of changeling dragons are BMW, Netflix and Starbucks. They watch, test, adapt, retool, and evolve as single entities. Their adaptive process tends to be linear, making their evolution easy to plot along a timeline. They don't necessarily branch out or diversify. They don't usually colonize either. They stick to the one market they dominate, watch over their turf and ward off would-be challengers by making sure to always be one big step ahead.

The second kind of dragon is the *seeding dragon*. The seeding dragon tends to drive innovation through an ecosystem of internal startups (and the occasional acquisition, as the need arises). In other words, it lays eggs and nurtures them. Examples of seeding dragons are Sony, Samsung and Alphabet (Google's parent company). Unlike changeling dragons, which tend to focus on a single industry (like automotive, entertainment or coffee), seeding dragons colonize. They diversify and branch out into more than one product category or market. Their adaptive process looks more like a tree than a single line, and is rooted in the startup spirit we typically think of when we talk about Silicon Valley.

Whichever type, *changeling* or *seeding*, a dragon happens to be, it is important to note that, eggs or not, like its reptilian cousins, a dragon can only grow by continuously shedding its old skin. This evolutionary trait forces it to exist in a constant state of renewal.

Two quick observations: The first is that this drives an instinctive need in dragons to continuously retread and breathe new life into their affairs. The second is that dragons benefit from a natural aversion to holding on to what they no longer need.

These traits don't come naturally to most established businesses—shedding old business models, products and ideas regularly, just like old skins, to grow bigger, stronger, faster and ultimately achieve market dominion. This may seem counterintuitive to companies whose success was built on iconic products and proven models. Replacing them with newer and potentially better ones is risky. What if they don't work? What about the threat of product cannibalization? Is it really wise to innovate and compete against yourself? These are all valid questions.

What makes dragons a little different from other companies is that they instinctively know that if they succumb to complacency and don't shed their skins regularly, no matter how successful they may have been for a time, they will slowly choke and die. A dragon knows that, once it's time to shed an old skin, it needs to shed it and move on.

The good news is that not all dragons are born. Dragons can be made. They can be *built*. Any company, given the will and the tools, can transform itself into a dragon if it wants to. *Changeling* or *seeding*, it doesn't matter. What matters is that this transformation is possible and within reach. This book's purpose is to introduce you to the basic vehicles for, and building blocks of, that change, and to help you make them work together so your company can ultimately become a dragon. As two of the most critical vehicles for this change are digital transformation and the rise of the experience economy, we will start there.

CHAPTER 1:

DIGITAL TRANSFORMATION AND BUSINESS DARWINISM FOR THE REAL WORLD

Please be sure to read the introduction before starting Chapter One, as it goes over important definitions that you will need to get the most out of this book.

When Jim Keyes, then CEO of Blockbuster Video, explained in a 2010 interview with *Fast Company* that Blockbuster, which, at the time, was sitting on 45 percent of the video rental market in the U.S., had nothing to fear from Netflix, he was correct. [1] Sixty percent of the demand for movies focused on new releases, and Netflix, the king of long tail content, could not compete against the video rental giant in that category. Blockbuster already offered a mail rental service similar to Netflix. The only thing — at least in Keyes's mind — that Netflix still did better than Blockbuster was *search*. Blockbuster was there to stay, and small players like Netflix never would grow into real contenders, let alone market leaders in the video rental industry. Less than two years later, Blockbuster was dethroned and all but gone.

Today, Netflix, which Blockbuster declined to purchase in 2000 for a mere $50 million, is a $30 billion empire. In early 2016, it announced the rollout of its services to 130 countries, and it isn't inconceivable that it could reach the 100 million subscriber mark by 2020.

¹Carr, A. (2010, June 08). Blockbuster CEO Jim Keyes on Competition From Apple, Netflix, Nintendo, and Redbox. http://www.fastcompany.com/1656502/blockbuster-ceo-jim-keyes-competition-apple-netflix-nintendo-and-redbox

In terms of reversals of fortune and market upheavals, it doesn't get much more dramatic than that. So, what happened?

If you asked hockey legend Wayne Gretzky, he might say Blockbuster was too busy focusing on where the puck was when it should have focused on where the puck was going to be.

To be fair, hockey isn't nearly as complex as making long-term business bets, but, in hindsight, Blockbuster appears to have ignored most of the signs that the movie rental industry was about to change. Instead, Blockbuster seemed more focused on maintaining the status quo than on pioneering new revenue models or shedding its old skin. The company failed to invest in new technologies (seeding innovation) or in its own transformation. Blockbuster still could be a successful company today had its leadership only had the right "adapt or die" mindset.

Business Darwinism, like every other type of Darwinism, isn't really about *survival of the fittest*. At its market apex, Blockbuster was as fit as a company can be. All incumbents are. What killed Blockbuster had nothing to do with being the fittest. It was its inability to adapt. *Adaptability* is the trait that determines survival. Business Darwinism is about *survival of the most adaptable*. This is our starting point. Before we tackle any other subject in this book, before we can even discuss digital transformation and the experience economy, we have to start here with this — your business's survival is dependent entirely on the speed with which it can adapt to change, which requires three types of action: 1) *Sensing* that change is coming, 2) *acknowledging* that change is coming and 3) *doing* something about it. In today's world, a business that cannot adapt quickly enough (or refuses to do so) will not survive.

DEFINING DIGITAL TRANSFORMATION

One of the biggest changes brought about by the digital era is a shift in the balance of power between businesses that *offer* products and services, and customers who *demand* products and services.

Customer expectations have changed. Obstacles that once protected incumbent companies from competition have all but been erased by the rise of social media and digital commerce. Loyalty can no longer be assumed; it has to be earned with every customer interaction. Before we can even talk about big data, mobile and other areas of focus we will cover in later chapters, we have to establish the understanding that digital has changed the power dynamic between companies and customers, and companies must adapt to this change.

When we talk about digital transformation, we are referring to a method of adapting to the new and ever changing digital economy, not just to survive (which is a great place to start), but to thrive. An effective digital transformation shouldn't be seen as an obstacle or a chore. It should be seen as an opportunity to gain a significant advantage over your competitors and take a leadership position in your industry or market. Yes, change is difficult, but it's a lot easier and far more rewarding when you take charge of it. What you don't want is to let change control you. That never ends well. (Ask Blockbuster how it worked out for them.)

When we reference digital transformation, we are talking about turning disruption from a *threat* into an *advantage*. First, this requires the right kind of mindset: Change is necessary. Change is good. Change is growth. For businesses to thrive and grow, they must evolve. To evolve, they need to be alert, innovative and agile.

Second, since innovation finds its purpose in change, and change requires agility to stick, a CEO has to ensure that his or her organization is built to be alert, innovative and agile. This is a core trait for any company looking to build long-term success.

To illustrate, let's return to our example:

Was Blockbuster alert, innovative and agile? No. Was Netflix alert, innovative and agile? Yes. The lesson practically teaches itself.

The ultimate objective of a company's digital transformation is to reach a point where it doesn't have to worry about being disrupted anymore. It can not only see change coming but *be* the change. It can take charge of its market or industry by disrupting it on a regular basis through a consistent stream of innovation that always puts it one step ahead of its competitors.

The alternative is to allow a competitor or outlier to disrupt its market or industry through an onslaught of innovation that leaves it battered, bruised and forced to mostly play defense. No competent CEO can possibly want that. The idea is to be Netflix, not Blockbuster. You want to be the disruptor, never the disrupted. If our original mantra was adapt or die, our new one is *take charge or suffer the consequences*.

What consequences? Well, being an also-in company doesn't quite cut it the way it used to. In most industries, market share is steered aggressively toward the top of the heap. The further down you fall in the pecking order, the less chance you have of still being in business three years from now. The days of sitting back and cruising comfortably by on 3 percent market share are over.

We are close to *take charge or die*. If taking charge of your industry is too overwhelming right this second, at least think about taking charge of your own company's destiny. *Take charge of your company's direction or die*. In the digital age, this doesn't just mean making your company adaptable to changes in your market. That's still far too reactive. It means making your company adaptable to opportunities that no one else has spotted yet. Yes, there is a difference — a big one. *Be the disruptor, not the disrupted.*

Digital transformation then, becomes the means by which your company will engineer its own competitive advantage. It is a platform for initiative, innovation and disruption.

CHAOTIC DISRUPTION VS. INTELLIGENT DISRUPTION

As much as we hear about disruption these days — either as a business model (which it isn't), a business strategy (which it is) or a market dynamic (and it most certainly is that) — disruption for disruption's sake brings little value to a market.

Think about a classroom, for instance. Fifty students sit at their desks, trying to learn the day's lesson. One student starts being disruptive to monopolize everyone's attention. Few students, teachers or onlookers would find that kind of self-serving disruption inspired or valuable. The same kind of chaotic disruption can be found in the business world, and its value is precisely zero. Companies that create disruption for its own sake may get a lot of attention for a short time, but the impact of that disruption on their own enterprise will be short lived and paper thin. In most cases, that type of disruption even will have a detrimental effect on the industry it "disrupted," as its overall stability and credibility will be shaken in the eyes of investors and customers. Instead of moving that industry forward and improving its value proposition, it will raise uncomfortable questions about what the future has in store for it.

Now compare chaotic disruption with intelligent disruption. In our classroom scenario, an example of intelligent disruption would be a student raising her hand to ask a question that alters the lecture and the students' understanding of the insights and lessons it might offer. An entirely new perspective on the topic of the lecture might suddenly emerge. Unexpected questions and conversations may arise as a result. What was boring one minute might become exciting and rewarding the next. When you look at disruption through this new lens, the difference between disruption for disruption's sake and disruption as an evolutionary leap is obvious.

In the business world, *intelligent disruption* is never disruption for disruption's sake either. It always results in an evolutionary leap. It either improves on an imperfect system or sends a particular category of product or service in a bold new direction.

INTELLIGENT DISRUPTION: THE NETFLIX REVOLUTION

Netflix wasn't chaotic in its disruption. Netflix saw an imperfect system in Blockbuster's video rental model. First, getting around Blockbuster's late fees (a pain point) was the original catalyst for Netflix. Second, Netflix sought to make rentals easier by allowing consumers to rent videos without having to leave their homes (another pain point). Netflix's intelligent disruption meant to improve on an imperfect system to:

• Reduce friction,
• Eliminate the risk of late fees,
• Be less time-consuming for customers, and
• Be more convenient for customers.

But Netflix didn't stop there. Even though mailing rentals back and forth was an improvement on the traditional rental model, it still was burdensome. There had to be a better, faster, cheaper, and more frictionless way to get content to their customers. It wasn't long before they found it. Seeing an opportunity in the growth of bandwidth usage by consumers, Netflix made a bet on the evolving economies of scale of data storage, download speeds and consumer-facing technologies. Netflix retooled, built a new operational model and started testing online content delivery that allowed customers to stream their rentals directly via the Internet.

Although we take Netflix for granted today, their model was extremely disruptive for its time. So disruptive, in fact, that it accelerated Blockbuster's demise and radically changed the video rental industry.

The shift from mail rentals to live streaming of content initially fell into the "improving an imperfect system" category of disruption. As before, the new model aimed to:

- Reduce friction,
- Eliminate late fees,
- Be less time-consuming for customers, and
- Be more convenient for customers.

This is same principle as before, right? Only this time, by innovating faster than its competitors, Netflix also managed to satisfy the second aspect of intelligent disruption. It created a new evolutionary branch of products and services. It then capitalized on that new direction by making these changes its principal market differentiator, then beating the market by *owning* that differentiator. Netflix wasn't just an *also-in service*, Netflix made itself the pioneer and the category leader.

Netflix continues to redefine its model to this day. The next step in the company's evolution was to borrow a strategy from the premium cable TV model and create original content instead of just being a content distributor. In many ways, Netflix became a lot more like an HBO than a Blockbuster. Although you might initially think that copying a mature entertainment channel model isn't particularly innovative or disruptive, remember that Netflix lives outside of the "cable company" ecosystem. Netflix and its audiences are not beholden to cumbersome third parties like cable companies. Anyone with an Internet connection and a device capable of streaming online video can become a Netflix customer. The disruption caused by that particular phase in Netflix's evolution — independent streaming services — was the beginning of TV watchers untethering themselves from cable companies.

We could continue with our Netflix example, but our discussion isn't really about Netflix. What we really are talking about is the combination of the purpose, the value and the processes behind the digital transformation of organizations in the experience economy. Before we go on, we need to get a clear sense of what these three aspects — purpose, value and process — really mean.

To recap, intelligent disruption typically serves two purposes:

1. It improves upon an imperfect system and/or
2. It creates a new evolutionary branch for a particular category of product or service.

WHAT, THEN, IS THE PURPOSE OF A DIGITAL TRANSFORMATION?

We understand now that the purpose of driving a company's digital transformation can be motivated by two things:

1. Survival and/or
2. Market Dominance.

That's it. There is no third motivation. The type of change we discuss in this book cannot be driven by a desire to follow industry trends, keep up with competitors or *"be disruptive."* Those methods aren't good enough. It is *vital* for you to understand that what we are talking about is a *necessary* form of adaptation specifically tailored to an increasingly digitally savvy and seamless experience-seeking market.

Survival (defensive posture) - if your company wants to still be in business five years from now, it needs to choose to be and focus on the correct strategies and investments.

Market dominance (offensive posture) - if your company wants to be the leader in its market five years from now, it needs to choose to be and focus on the correct strategies and investments.

Bear in mind that 50 percent of companies listed on the Fortune 500 in 1995 are no longer on it today. Some just got smaller and fell off the list, while others evaporated into the vortex that is digital disruption.

WHAT IS THE VALUE OF A DIGITAL TRANSFORMATION IN THE EXPERIENCE ECONOMY?

You now understand the value of digital transformation to the organization itself (survival and/or market dominance), but these are relatively vague objectives. Let's consider more specific values that can result from a digital transformation mindset. Think of them as the building blocks of your organization's value for the next five, 10 and 15 years (and hopefully beyond). Here are some common examples from companies already deploying digital transformation strategies across their business:

- Friction-free interactions with customers,
- Seamless shopping experiences from discovery to delivery,

- Higher transaction velocity,
- Lower operating costs,
- Lower customer erosion rates,
- Higher loyalty and repeat business from existing customers,
- Higher rates of referrals and recommendations from customers,
- High customer satisfaction ratings,
- High employee satisfaction ratings,
- Higher quality of job applicants,
- Increased sales volume,
- Greater market share,
- More opportunities for advantageous strategic partnerships,
- More opportunities for strategic acquisitions,
- Faster adaptation to new technologies, and
- Faster identification and leveraging of emerging market opportunities.

Because value is never so clear as when it is weighed against costs, here are the costs of not committing to this type of adaptation:

- Friction-laden interactions with customers,
- Inconsistent and disappointing shopping experiences for customers,
- Lower transaction velocity,
- High operating costs,
- High customer erosion rates,
- Low loyalty and little repeat business from existing customers,
- Lower rates of referrals and recommendations from customers,
- Low customer satisfaction ratings,
- High employee turnover rate,
- Lower quality of job applicants,
- Lower sales volume,
- Lower/Lost market share,
- Less opportunities for strategic partnerships,
- Less opportunities for strategic acquisitions,
- Difficulty adapting to new technologies, and
- Difficulty identifying and leveraging new market opportunities.

Hint: One of these two lists is a lot better than the other. Which do you prefer?

WHAT ARE THE PROCESSES BEHIND DIGITAL TRANSFORMATIONS IN THE EXPERIENCE ECONOMY?

We will discuss processes and best practices throughout this book, but what is important to understand at this juncture is that there *is* a methodology that makes this all possible, and any organization that follows its principles should adapt to change, anticipate change and turn that change into a competitive advantage, just like Netflix, Amazon, Google, Apple, and other industry leaders. Helping you understand the *why*, *what* and *how* of this process is the purpose of this book.

THE SEVEN LAWS OF DIGITAL TRANSFORMATION:

1. The entire customer experience must be at the heart of digital transformation.
2. When we talk about *customer experience*, we are talking about a *buyer's journey*. Every buyer's journey starts with discovery and a subsequent first interaction.
3. Remember that the buyer's journey includes customer reviews and ratings.
4. All touchpoints must be remarkable and impactful.
5. All customer experiences must be simple, intuitive, frictionless, and personal.
6. All customer experiences must drive future interactions and inspire loyalty.
7. All customer touchpoints must be integrated across all platforms.

INFLECTION POINTS AND THE VIRTUE OF KILLING YOUR BUSINESS TO SAVE YOUR BUSINESS

Digital transformation starts with the fear of alienating current users by changing too much, too quickly. Your customers are the foundation of your business, so you want to make sure they are happy. Kodak and Blackberry are great examples of companies trying to stay in the past while simultaneously meeting the future. The problem isn't so much that this model is difficult to pull off. The problem is that sometimes, by holding on to the past, companies end up holding on to the wrong things for what they *think* are the right reasons.

As we explained in the preface, dragons are companies that adapt and evolve to disrupt their markets. Old skin (outdated habits and processes) must be shed to evolve. It's just that more often than not, old skin often retains the look and feel of past successes. That can be confusing if you don't naturally have a dragon's shedding instinct. For most executives, it's hard to see past what is merely an afterglow of success. It's even harder to let go of cash cows, no matter how tired and outdated they may be.

Dragons and dragon builders, because, as we explained previously, dragons can be made, know better than to succumb to the fear of disrupting their own model. They understand that shedding old skins is the only way to grow. Letting go is just a normal step in their cycle of growth. To become a dragon, you have to trust in the process and keep moving forward.

In *Only the Paranoid Survive: How to Identity and Exploit the Crisis Points that Challenge Every Business*, Andy Grove, former CEO of Intel, talks about the importance of spotting what he calls "inflection points." [2]

An *inflection point* is where you know the industry your business operates in has changed so profoundly that you can either change your business completely or get killed by your competitors. The inflection could be a change in competition, regulatory issues or technology. Grove believed in taking action, doing something about it, staying ahead of times, and winning at all cost, even if it meant changing even his company's core areas of business. According to Grove, "most companies don't die because they are wrong; most die because they don't commit themselves. They fritter away their valuable resources while attempting to make a decision. The greatest danger is in standing still." [3]

NO CRYSTAL BALL? NO PROBLEM.

The cluster of questions we are all asking ourselves is "How could anyone at Blockbuster know what was coming? How could their executives have known that new technologies would transform their business model, let alone what these technologies would be? In other words, short of having a crystal ball, how could they have seen what was coming?"

There is no way to know what is coming. Not for sure. Great companies make bad bets all the time. Sometimes they make the right bets

---

[2]Grove, A. S. (1996). *Only the paranoid survive: How to exploit the crisis points that challenge every company and career.* New York: Currency Doubleday.
[3]Grove, A. S. (1996). *Only the paranoid survive: How to exploit the crisis points that challenge every company and career.* New York: Currency Doubleday.

too early, they don't execute on some critical aspect of their product lifecycle properly or they quit trying too quickly. The most innovative companies in the world — Google, Microsoft, Sony, and even Apple — make mistakes regularly. What makes them successful in spite of this?

- There is a difference between testing new products and services, and radically changing your business model overnight.

When Microsoft got into the media player game in 2006 with Zune, the project did not threaten its other product lines. It wasn't a replacement for anything. It was a new product for a new market (much like Xbox was). Zune was a great product for its time, and, in many ways, superior to the iPod. Sadly, Microsoft wasn't able to build a retail presence around Zune that could compete with what Apple was doing for iPod. It also wasn't able to build as seamless a user experience (the Zune store, for instance) as Apple. Microsoft could have fixed these weaknesses, but, instead of listening to its market, engaging with its core users, and working to improve the Zune ecosystem's weaknesses, it gave up (many might say too quickly).

Given how Apple used the iPod Touch as a platform for the iPhone, and seeing how iPhone transformed the world (and Apple), one can look back at Microsoft's decision to kill Zune as one of the tech world's most short-sighted business decisions of all time (which is a lesson in itself). Even though Microsoft's decision to kill Zune effectively put it years behind in what eventually became the smartphone industry, the missed opportunity did not hurt Microsoft's core businesses. Sales of its other products and services trended as expected. Zune's death was a non-event. It didn't throw the company into financial upheaval.

It is only in hindsight that you can see where Microsoft decision-makers, had they given more thought to where the puck was going to be rather than where the puck was, could have used Zune to give iPhone a run for its money right from the start.

- "Fail faster, succeed sooner." - David Kelley, Founder of IDEO
Missed opportunities are always tragic, but you can't dwell on what could have been or should have been. You either fix your mistakes as they come and keep going, or leave your regrets in the past where they belong. One thing you will notice about companies that innovate (and become good at it) is that they learn to fail faster than their competitors.

What does that mean? Think about the time it takes to come up with an idea, design it, prototype it, test it, measure its success, consider its potential, and decide whether to continue driving it forward. Ten years ago, the process could take up to 18 months to complete — 18 months of product development and testing to discover if your new product *might* be successful. Today that timeframe would make your product obsolete before it even got to market.

Now consider three companies all working on a similar idea. Company A completes the prototyping and testing process in 12 months. Company B completes the process in six months. Company C completes the process in three months. Which one do you think has the advantage? That's right. Company C. Why? Because whether the idea was good or bad, it will know faster than its competitors.

If the idea is good, it can use feedback from its testers and early adopters to make critical improvements to its product quickly and keep building on its initial success.

If the idea is bad, it invested only three months into the project and can start work on its next idea. (A three month project lifecycle means Company C can go through this process four times in one year, while Company B can only produce and test two ideas per year, and Company A only one.)

Bonus: While companies A and B waste time testing their ideas, Company C already has either gone to market with an increasingly successful product, or stopped wasting time and resources, and moved on to test the next big idea.

The company with the most streamlined idea-to-prototype-to-testing process has the advantage because:

- It will be the fastest to innovate and identify new ways of generating revenue.
- It will spend the least amount of funding to test new ideas.
- It will move its market forward with new products, new solutions and new services.
- It will have the initiative, which means it will set the rules when it comes to setting new standards of quality, efficiency, etc.

Examples of companies that test small and fast are Amazon, Google and Facebook. Granted, software is a lot easier to optimize than space rockets (although that is changing, as we will discuss later in the book), but that is kind of the point. Technology, particularly software and software-based products and services, provides the fastest and most cost-effective avenues for innovation and forward momentum available to any organization today — not new manufacturing techniques, investing in new tooling, hiring a new shipping company, or spending more on retail placement.

It also doesn't matter much if your company sells artisan chocolates, athletic shoes, bicycles, or professional services. The primary game-changer — the *force multiplier* — is effective integration of the right tech into every aspect of your business, from customer-facing touchpoints and internal collaboration to product management and market research. This, perhaps above all other reasons listed in these chapters, is why focusing on digital transformation is so vital to companies today. Digital transformation bears the lowest cost and yields the highest return of any investment you can make in your company's future.

CHAPTER 2:

WHAT IS *EXPERIENCE ECONOMY*, AND WHY DOES IT MATTER?

The notion of an *experience economy* first started catching on in the 1970s thanks to futurist Alvin Toffler. Toffler imagined that consumer needs and desires, fueled by a shift toward a post-industrial society (in which most goods would become disposable and buying would be replaced by renting), would evolve beyond traditional models of utility, scarcity and value. He laid out this idea in his best-selling book *Future Shock*, predicting that future consumers' value systems would shift away from merely paying for quality *products* to paying for *experiences*, and the more amazing the experience, the better. [4]

German sociologist Gerhard Schulze took these ideas a step further 20 years later in his book *The Experience Society* [5]. Schulze's predictions were echoed by Rolf Jensen, director of the Copenhagen Institute for Future Studies, in his book, *The Dream Society* [6], then B. Joseph Pine and James Gilmore in their book *The Experience Economy.* [7]

[4]Toffler, A. (1970). *Future shock*. New York: Random House.
[5]Schulze, G. (2005). *The experience society*. London: Sage.
[6]Jensen, R. (1999). *The dream society: How the coming shift from information to imagination will transform your business*. New York: McGraw-Hill.
[7]Pine, B. J., & Gilmore, J. H. (1999). *The experience economy: Work is theatre & every business a stage*. Boston: Harvard Business School Press.

Though the socioeconomic context of these predictions are deep and far-reaching, especially given how accurate they were many years before the digital revolution really took off, the concept of creating value through delightful experiences is nothing new, evidenced by traditional adages like "the customer is king." At the heart of that universal customer service philosophy lies the fundamental understanding that, for businesses to be successful, customers expect not only positive experiences but *remarkable* ones. What was once merely a question of asking "how can we gain a slight advantage over our competition by treating our customers well (or creating delightful experiences for them)?" morphed into something much bigger, much more mission-critical, more *deliberate* than *haphazard* and more measurable science than intangible dark art.

DEFINING THE EXPERIENCE ECONOMY

What then is the experience economy? How is it defined? Is it something that, as business leaders and consumers, we can actually see, touch or feel? How tangible is it, really?

The first step in understanding the experience economy as defined by Pine and Gilmore is to acknowledge that *experiences* are a distinct economic offering, just like *commodities*, *goods* and *services*. [8] In fact, Pine and Gilmore go as far as to graph the progression of economic value thus:

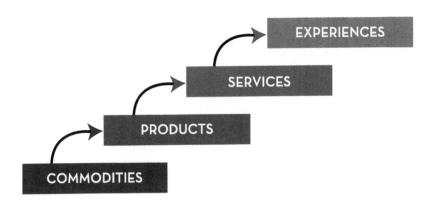

Fig. 2.1: **Progression of Economic Value**

---

[8]Pine, B. J., & Pine, B. J., & Gilmore, J. H. (1999). *The experience economy: Work is theatre & every business a stage.* Boston: Harvard Business School Press.

Second, Pine and Gilmore explain that "an experience is not an amorphous construct; it is as real an offering as any service, good, or commodity." Third, as economic offerings, *experiences* are as different from *services* as *services* are from *goods*. As they explain it, "commodities are *fungible*, goods are *tangible*, services are *intangible*, and experiences are memorable." [9]

Even without a thorough understanding of economics, we can understand the value and markets for these offerings by thinking of simple examples they naturally evoke for us. For commodities (like steel and grain), we likely visualize large shipping operations and industrial marketplaces, and we understand the role they play in our everyday lives. For goods, it's grocery stores, shopping malls, Amazon, your closet shelves, your pantry, etc. Easy enough, right? For the less tangible *service economy*, we can visualize how we value restaurants, hotels, taxis, and so on. Visualizing the value of experiences is no different. Obvious examples of the experience economy include watching a movie, attending a concert, swimming with dolphins, and touring the Eiffel Tower.

Once you understand these basic constructs, the question becomes this: How does this apply to my company, which sells products or services, instead of experiences? What does watching movies and skiing in Vail have to do with what *we* do? Pine and Gilmore's answer lies in four words: *staging experiences that sell*. Here is how they define the process: "An experience occurs when a company intentionally uses services as the stage, and goods as props, to engage individual customers in a way that creates a memorable event." [10]

An example that Pine and Gilmore are fond of is an episode of the old television show *Taxi*, in which one of the characters, Iggy, decides to become the best cab driver in the world. To attain this goal, Iggy serves his customers snacks and drinks, takes them on tours of the city, and even treats them to renditions of Frank Sinatra songs. Here is their take on that episode:

"By engaging passengers in a way that turned an ordinary cab ride into a memorable event, Iggy created something else entirely — a distinct economic offering. The *experience* of riding in his cab was more valuable to his customers than the service of being transported by the cab — and in the TV show, at least, Iggy's customers happily responded by giving bigger tips. By asking to go around the block again, one patron even *paid more* for poorer service just to prolong his enjoyment. The

---

[9]Pine, B. J., & Gilmore, J. H. (1999). *The experience economy: Work is theatre & every business a stage.* Boston: Harvard Business School Press.
[10]Pine, B. J., & Gilmore, J. H. (1999). *The experience economy: Work is theatre & every business a stage.* Boston: Harvard Business School Press.

service Iggy provided — taxi transportation — was simply the stage for the experience that he was really selling." [11]

What does this teach us? First, it gives us a better glimpse into what experience as an offering actually is. Second, it gives us valuable insight into how experiences can be integrated into an existing business model (remember the *stage and props* equation). Third, and this may be the most important lesson, customers *will* buy experiences. In other words, given the opportunity, customers will become *buyers of experiences*.

The experience economy, therefore, is an economy, or rather a market, that connects *sellers of experiences* and *buyers of experiences*.

Close your eyes. Think of the excitement of Christmas morning when you were a kid. Think of how amazing it feels to take your first gulp of a cold drink after having worked hard in your yard on a hot summer day. Think of the excitement of unboxing something you have waited months or weeks to finally receive. The experience economy is rooted in these moments and the value of these emotions, but it also extends to thousands of smaller experiences (one might call them micro-experiences) that add up to create lasting impressions of brands.

From delighting customers to eliminating every pain point between discovery and repeat purchases (no matter how small), the experience economy is driven by an understanding that, to win new customers *and* earn their undying loyalty, the most effective strategy is to become known for consistently delivering the best experiences of any company in your market. (How pleasant, delightful or fun is the shopping experience? How easy is it for customers to find what they are looking for? How painless is it to check out? How easy is it to start using the product?) Doing this right requires deliberate effort and an adequate focus on *customer experience management*, which starts and ends with *customer experience design*.

FROM DARK ART TO SCIENCE: THE ROI CASE FOR CUSTOMER EXPERIENCE DESIGN

Walk into any successful retail space today and customer *experience design* is everywhere. The storefront itself, the way you are greeted by the staff, the store's layout, the lighting, the way the store smells, the ambient music, the texture of everything you are meant to touch, the fitting room, the checkout, even the bag you carry your items out with are all part of the experience. Every touchpoint is designed to delight, amaze, make you feel special (and good about your purchase), and to make you excited at the

---

[11]Pine, B. J., & Gilmore, J. H. (1999). *The experience economy: Work is theatre & every business a stage*. Boston: Harvard Business School Press.

thought of coming back, hopefully with a friend. None of it is an accident.

Fun fact: Up to 95 percent of purchase triggers are subconscious [12]. Because retailers know this, they have invested millions in research to determine how their stores should feel, smell and sound to 1) improve customer experiences, 2) make customers want to stay in the store as long as possible (there is a direct correlation between time spent in a store and the amount of money a shopper spends), 3) trigger purchases, and 4) make them want to keep coming back.

One of the most important aspects of customer experience design is the ability to test and measure investments against business objectives. (In other words, determining the ROI of every experience design element a retailer might want to spend resources on.) For instance, what impact would additional mirrors throughout the store have on average customer spend per visit? This is measurable. It can be tested and quantified. A retailer can find out fairly quickly whether stores with more mirrors perform better than they used to *and* better than other stores.

This focus on *purpose* and *measurable effect* is a far more effective than the traditional way of approaching retail design, which would have amounted to simply listening to a designer's suggestion that adding more mirrors would make the store seem bigger and more upscale. While those insights may be true, they don't exactly help answer the real question: "How will this help our business be more successful?"

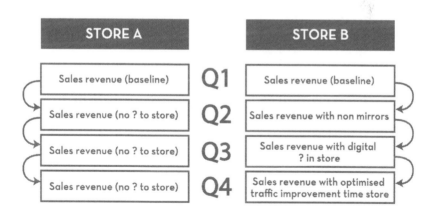

Fig. 2.2: **A/B Testing: Experience Design**

[12]Pradeep, A. K. (2010). *The buying brain: Secrets for selling to the subconscious mind.* Hoboken, NJ: Wiley.

To illustrate the potential value of experience design, let's briefly look at a 1993 study by neurologist Dr. Alan Hirsch. His work paved the way for most of the experience design practices that we use today.

Hirsch's theory was that even something as subtle as smell could have a profound influence on retail customer behaviors. To prove this, he and his team devised a simple experiment. They placed two identical pairs of Nike shoes in two identical rooms. The only difference between them — one room was unscented while the other was lightly scented with a mixed floral fragrance. The result: A whopping 84 percent of shoppers who took part in the experiment reported feeling more desire for the pair of shoes in the scented room. (Bonus: These shoppers also expected the value of the shoes displayed in the scented room to be $10 higher than the pair in the unscented room and *still* wanted them.) [13]

It isn't difficult to imagine how much of a game changer it would be to show a retail CEO that a small investment in something as simple as a store fragrance could a) significantly increase sales and b) even have a positive impact on the price elasticity of certain products. Thus, the case could be made that something as simple and inexpensive as making your espresso-maker stores smell like coffee beans, your lingerie stores smell like lilac, and your baby superstores smell like baby powder could result in tens of millions of dollars in *net new* annual revenue. This type of experience design doesn't need to be limited to retail either. Service and technology companies can focus on a 100 percent digital customer journey design that will yield improved conversion rates and increase customer satisfaction.

What is most fascinating about this *specific* aspect of experience design though, isn't that it has widespread applications. It isn't that it has measurable impact either. And it isn't even that, since smells can trigger powerful emotions (like security, desire, comfort, hunger, thirst, courage, excitement, nostalgia, loyalty, and love), retail experiences can be designed to trigger and reinforce particular behaviors in shoppers. The most fascinating thing about it is, for all the potential that olfactory experience design brings to the table, *smell* accounts for less than 1 percent of a shopper's overall buying decisions.

That's it.

Olfactory experience design, by itself and for all its potential, is little more than the thin frosty layer atop the tip of an iceberg that also encompasses senses like sight, sound, touch, and taste, but also expectations, assumptions, memories, beliefs, biases, and so on (emotional and psychological triggers that transcend brick and mortar

---

[13]Hirsch, A. R., Hirsch, A. R., & Hirsch, A. R. (1996). *Articles dealing with the effect of aroma on human behavior*. Chicago, IL: Smell & Taste Treatment and Research Foundation.

retail environments). That's important because now that we understand the *where*, *how* and *why* of how customer experience design grew into the science it has become, we have a foundation upon which to build our understanding of how it also fits into the omnichannel* marketplaces** of the digital age, where the experience economy lives and breathes.

* Omnichannel marketplaces - both *digital-only* marketplaces and hybrid digital/non-digital marketplaces.

** Note that by "marketplaces" we aren't just talking about transactional channels like online stores and mobile shopping carts. We also are referencing marketplaces for ideas and opinions (social media), consumer review channels (like *Yelp!*), search engines, digital and mobile advertising channels, and so on.

THE DIFFERENCE BETWEEN REINVENTING THE WHEEL AND LETTING IT COME FULL CIRCLE

None of this is new. Enjoying a delicious meal at a restaurant, marveling at how comfortable a pair of boots still is, admiring the expert craftsmanship of pretty much any product... remarkable, memorable experiences are what good business has always been about.

It's just that the industrial revolution shifted the economics of value from quality to affordability, which is to say that it created a new value model that tended to favor the efficiency of *mass production* and *mass distribution* over the creation of genuine, authentic and memorable experiences. The few companies that managed to weave industrial efficiency and product quality to create the right balance of accessibility and memorable experiences stood out against a market filled with more utility than delight, and those companies were handsomely rewarded for their inspired approach. Among the early pioneers of this hybrid model were Ford, Coca Cola and Disney. Their success paved the way for companies like Nike, Apple, Harley Davidson, Starbucks, and BMW.

The lesson is that we *always* have lived in an experience economy. The push toward *humanizing* companies again and injecting products, brands and interactions with *authenticity* in recent years is symptomatic of a natural need to restore the balance between industrial efficiency (cost-effectiveness, velocity, frictionless touchpoints, and scale), and pleasant-to-remarkable experiences. Also, much of this can and should be attributed to the impact that digital is having on consumption. Hence, the urgency to digitally transform.

BUT WHAT DOES ANY OF THIS HAVE TO DO WITH DIGITAL TRANSFORMATION?

At the World Economic Forum's 2016 Annual Meeting in Davos, Switzerland, Pierre Nanterme, CEO of Accenture, reminded business and world leaders that *"digital is the main reason just over half of the companies on the Fortune 500 have disappeared since the year 2000. [14]"* He's right. Yes, that is a shocking statistic, but the real question is: *Why is digital so important?*

The answer is twofold:

1. As we just discussed, no company can hope to remain competitive for long without becoming an active player in the experience economy.
2. No company can hope to be competitive in the experience economy without creating for itself the best possible digital ecosystem.

Digital transformation must therefore not be driven by an abstract need to "get more digital" or "remain competitive in the digital era" (which look great on paper but mean nothing), but by a clear sense of strategic purpose. For instance, evolving from merely being a *products* and *services* company to becoming an *experiences* company.

One could also cite dozens of other reasons to embrace digital (improving customer service, doing more with data, improving customer engagement, etc.), but it is clear that all of these strategic initiatives are about "doing things better" or "becoming a better company," which fit within the scope of creating better experiences for customers. In other words, every trigger driving the need for your organization to embrace a digital transformation is rooted in the experience economy. Once you realize that, it's a lot easier to see the whole board.

The reason this chapter is twice as long as any other is because of how *important* it is that you understand how and why your market is changing, how the *experience economy* plays into this massive change, and why digital transformation is the key to survive this change and thrive from it.

* Moore's Law - based on Intel founder Gordon Moore's 1965 prediction that the number of components on integrated circuits could be expected to double without increasing in cost about every two years. [15] (The simple version: Computers keep getting smaller, faster and

[14]Natnterme, P. (2016, January 16). Digital disruption has only just begun. https://www.weforum.org/agenda/2016/01/digital-disruption-has-only-just-begun
[15]Thackray, A., Brock, D. C., & Jones, R. (2015). *Moore's law: The life of Gordon Moore, Silicon Valley's quiet revolutionary.* New York, NY: Perseus Books.

cheaper.) Note that this brings us back to Alvin Toffler's prediction of a post-industrial economy, where even computers (perhaps *especially* computers) become disposable commodities. [16]

HOW THIS PLAYS IN DIGITAL AND OMNICHANNEL MARKETPLACES

We have talked about the importance of customer experience design for brick-and-mortar retailers. Let's talk about how it fits in both digital and omnichannel (hybrid digital and brick and mortar) marketplaces.

The numbers below help illustrate how much digital technology and mobility are radically changing the world we live in.

- By 2020, as much as 80 percent of all global media consumption will be digital (as opposed to 50 percent in 2000). [17]
- By 2020, average global media consumption will reach a whopping 80 to 100 hours per week. (More than twice the amount of hours the average full time employee spends at work.) [18]
- By 2020, 4.7 billion people (out of the world's projected population of 7.7 billion) will be connected to the Internet. (That's almost two thirds.) [19]
- By 2020, nearly all of the world's 4.7 billion Internet users will be accessing the Internet primarily through mobile devices. [20]
- Whether or not they actually have access to the Internet, by 2020, roughly six billion people around the world will be mobile users. [21]

Does this mean that consumers will no longer shop at brick and mortar retail stores? No. Does it mean they will stop going out for dinner or hanging out at coffee shops? No. Will they stop going to movies, plays and concerts? No. But the way they shop, the way they consume news and entertainment, the way they learn, the way they interact with their family, friends and peers, and every aspect of the way they shape and customize the world around them will be as deeply rooted in the digital

[16]Toffler, A. (1970). *Future shock*. New York: Random House.
[17]World Association of Newspapers. (2007-2008). Chart/table from: Newspapers Mull Future amid Digital Media Boom. http://www.marketingcharts.com/traditional/newspapers-mull-future-amid-digital-media-boom-4820/attachment/wan-global-media-consumption-per-week-by-mediumjpg/
[18]World Association of Newspapers. (2007-2008). Chart/table from: Newspapers Mull Future amid Digital Media Boom. http://www.marketingcharts.com/traditional/newspapers-mull-future-amid-digital-media-boom-4820/attachment/wan-global-media-consumption-per-week-by-mediumjpg/
[19]Friedrich, R., Peterson, M., Koster, A., & Blum, S. (2010). *The Rise of Generation C and Implications for the world of 2020* [PDF]. Booz & Company.
[20]Friedrich, R., Peterson, M., Koster, A., & Blum, S. (2010). *The Rise of Generation C and Implications for the world of 2020* [PDF]. Booz & Company.
[21]Friedrich, R., Peterson, M., Koster, A., & Blum, S. (2010). *The Rise of Generation C and Implications for the world of 2020* [PDF]. Booz & Company.

space as is their attention already. Companies have to not only be where their customers are, but they also have to be able to compete for their attention and their dollars on these digital channels.

This isn't just about *selling*. It isn't just an exercise in relocating or duplicating brick and mortar retail spaces in the digital world. Don't make the common mistake of losing your focus on selling experiences, not just products and services. Remember Pine and Gilmore's wise words: "An experience occurs when a company intentionally uses services as the stage, and goods as props, to engage individual customers in a way that creates a memorable event." [22]

The main difference between creating remarkable experiences at scale in the pre-digital era vs. the era of digital (especially as digital embeds itself into our everyday lives via connected devices, sensors, mobility, cloud, artificial intelligence, etc.) is that digital allows companies to create entire ecosystems of experiences for their customers (and employees) that were not technically possible, let alone cost-effective, in the pre-digital era. Thanks to a combination of modern computing, mobile technology, social channels, cloud computing, and access to data, a company's ability to design and deliver consistently remarkable and personalized experiences for their customers at scale and via any touchpoint in their business ecosystem is unparalleled.

Speaking of access data, one major piece of the digital transformation puzzle, especially as it relates to its role in the experience economy, touches on the way digital channels allow businesses to better understand their customers, predict their needs and wants, and customize solutions that will maximize purchase intent in the short term and loyalty in the long term. This is a topic we will get into a little more later on, but it is worth mentioning here.

Equally important are the financial and technical barriers of entry that existed even a decade ago — access to funding, technical knowledge, bandwidth, IT capacity, and so on — have all but flattened. Today, a small three-person startup in New Jersey, Oregon or Arizona can turn a simple idea into a Fortune 500 killer. Inattentive incumbent market leaders can easily find themselves dethroned in a matter of months without knowing what hit them.

In short, your ads, marketing, emails, and content can follow your customers all day and jump from their mobile devices to their computers to their tablets to their other connective devices without

[22]Pine, B. J., & Gilmore, J. H. (1999). *The experience economy: Work is theatre & every business a stage*. Boston: Harvard Business School Press.

ever being annoying or interruptive. Your storefront can live in their pockets, in their hands, on their desks, or pretty much anywhere. All of their shopping can be done in a matter of seconds and with little more than a few swipes of a finger. Insight into their tastes, preferences and behaviors takes the guesswork out of catering to their specific needs. Creating seamless and consistent experiences between your physical and virtual touchpoints no longer has to be a friction point between your customers' expectations and the reality of your customer experience ecosystem. This is the ultimate objective. This is the goal.

It isn't all about customers and marketplaces, by the way. Our broader digital transformation discussion *also* will touch on the ways in which technology impacts the nature of work (the way in which organizations operate). As we write this book, about 20 percent of work in the U.S. is done remotely [23], with 37 percent of employed adults reporting that they have telecommuted (worked from home using a computer). [24]

Those numbers could rise easily, as 50 percent of the U.S. workforce *already* has a job compatible with at least some degree of telecommuting. [25] Moreover, 41 percent of companies already rely on contingent employees. [26] How well prepared organizations are in terms of managing virtual teams and workforces is as important as everything else we have discussed thus far.

TAKEAWAYS, LESSONS AND INSIGHTS FROM THE TRENCHES

We want to share three crucial takeaways from what we have discussed thus far and add a little bit of helpful insight into this topic.

1. Customer experience design is not an abstraction. It is (more than *product design, competitive pricing,* and even *marketing spend*) the single most important competitive opportunity that companies

---

[23] Cocorocchia, C., El-Azar, D., Jentsch, A., Luo, M., O'Neil, A., & Woodward, L. (2016, January). Digital Media and Society - Section 4: Outlook and Call to Action. http://reports.weforum.org/human-implications-of-digital-media-2016/section-4-outlook-and-call-to-action/?doing_wp_cron=14590305 81.2192850112915039062500

[24] Jones, J. M. (2015, August 19). In U.S., Telecommuting for Work Climbs to 37%. http://www.gallup.com/poll/184649/telecommuting-work-climbs.aspx

[25] Lister, K., & GlobalWorkplaceAnalytics.com. (2016, January). Latest Telecommuting Statistics – Global Workplace Analytics. http://globalworkplaceanalytics.com/telecommuting-statistics

[26] Cocorocchia, C., El-Azar, D., Jentsch, A., Luo, M., O'Neil, A., & Woodward, L. (2016, January). Digital Media and Society – Benefits and Opportunities. http://reports.weforum.org/human-implications-of-digital-media-2016/benefits-and-opportunities

have at their disposal to remain competitive and take a leadership position in their markets.

2. Dollar for dollar, customer experience design offers the best risk-to-reward ratio of any investment aiming to help companies gain and maintain a significant advantage in their markets.

3. Focusing on the design and delivery of *experiences* rather than just products and services is the kind of holistic and inspired approach that has driven companies like BMW, Apple, Google, Sharpie, Starbucks, Netflix, Whole Foods, Zappos, and Virgin America to the top of their respective markets.

WHAT GOLF, SURFING AND YOUR MORNING COMMUTE CAN TEACH YOU ABOUT SHIFTING YOUR FOCUS.

A change of focus is much simpler and easier to accomplish than it might first seem. Becoming an experience-focused company doesn't mean you have to completely retool your business. You don't have to fire your staff or start doing everything differently. It isn't like that. All you have to do is change your perspective a tiny bit.

Becoming an experience-focused company starts by simply looking toward a slightly more distant horizon than the one you had your eyes on a month ago. That's all it is. By changing your paradigm, you allow your mind to shift from managing the complexity of a hundred moving parts to focusing on driving toward a single unified goal — delivering better experiences. This process doesn't complicate, it *simplifies*.

Once you are able to shift your focus forward, delivering extraordinary experiences will drive every part of your business — product design, customer service, marketing, advertising, shopping, logistics, IT, and so on. Once customer experience is identified as a priority, every part of your organization will align naturally to that priority.

To put this in perspective, let us connect this to something you already understand. There are hundreds of examples of how this process already turns up in everyday life — driving a car, riding a bike, running, surfing, playing tennis or golf. Here's how it works. First, when you are driving, your mind isn't constantly focused on where your hands are, the exact pressure of your foot on the pedal, the precise angle of the wheels relative to the road, etc. You're just driving. You're just focused on where you are going and every part of your body naturally aligns to that mission. Same with hitting a ball, riding a surfboard or doing any number of things in which series of complex movements all serve to accomplish a common goal. You don't have to overthink the hitting of the ball or the angle of the surfboard any more than you have to overthink the car's controls. In fact, the less you think about every detail, the smoother things go. The clearer your mind is, the more passively focused it is on where you want to go (or where you want the ball to go), the better. It's when you start thinking about the details that things start going sideways.

A simple fact of physics is that your eyes dictate where your body goes. Your eyes also dictate where your racket, bat, vehicle, or ball goes. We all know this. Mind, eyes, mind's eye… it's all the same thing. It all comes down to focus. Ironically, we all understand this about sports and driving and dozens of everyday things, but we often forget to apply the same logic and insights to the business world. We have a bit of a blind spot when it comes to connecting all of the dots. Let this be a reminder that you should connect those dots, because, if you do, everything becomes simpler.

The bottom line is that keeping your eyes on the target is good, and removing your eyes from the target is bad. This is no different. The same principle that makes you fall off your surfboard the second you start thinking about staying up will make you fail in business. The same principle that will make you slice your ball into the weeds the second you start focusing on your grip instead of where you want the ball to go will make you screw up in business. Look beyond the immediate set of obstacles or challenges that you *think* you need to address (things like revamping your content strategy again, meeting unrealistic online sales goals this month or tweaking your latest mobile ad campaign), and your momentum will carry you through. Focusing on creating amazing, memorable experiences for your customers and users will infuse every aspect of your business with clarity, purpose, direction, and momentum.

In summation, for best results, digital transformation and experience-centered design need to become entrenched in your culture, rather than being a checkbox item in your five-year business plan.

CHAPTER 3:

TYING DIGITAL TRANSFORMATION TO "REAL WORLD" BUSINESS OBJECTIVES

Now that we covered big topics like business Darwinism, digital transformation and the experience economy, let's spend a little time looking at how this all applies to your business.

First things first. It doesn't matter if your business is a 100-year-old enterprise with a global footprint, a 10-year-old medium-sized business with fewer than five locations, or a 3-month-old startup with a staff of three, most of the principles and insights shared in this book apply. How you decide to turn these insights into solutions will vary from business to business, but scale is merely a factor that makes Business A as different from Business B as it is different from Business C. At this juncture, our focus in teaching you the fundamentals of digital transformation is not to spend time on all the ways in which businesses may be different, but rather on all the ways that businesses are the same. Differences in size, industry and markets come later.

Second, let's bring this entire discussion down to a level that every CEO and business manager can relate to — actual business objectives.

DIGITAL TRANSFORMATION AS DRIVER OF BUSINESS OBJECTIVES

We aren't talking about digital transformation *vs.* other business objectives. Your current business objectives, short-term and long-term, should not compete *against* your organization's digital transformation.

"We're already too busy with other projects" or "our resources are already stretched too thin as it is" are natural and understandable reactions to the suggestion of a new focus for any company, but they suggest a fundamental misunderstanding of how digital transformation and business objectives work together rather than against one another.

"Digital transformation" is not just another item on your list of business objectives. Whatever budgets and resources you have allocated to existing initiatives will not have to be diverted or hijacked. Digital transformation is going to become a part of your business's *existing* objectives, just like those objectives are going to become part of your digital transformation. In other words, digital transformation is going to help you *achieve* and get *more* out of your existing objectives.

It is important to acknowledge that a digital transformation is not a distraction, a drain on resources or a strategic bet that can be put off until "later." Digital transformation is an enhancement of existing capabilities. In the military, this is what's commonly known as a *force-multiplier* - a factor that dramatically increases (multiplies) the effectiveness and potential of an item or group. The same concept applies here.

FROM SURVIVAL TO MARKET DOMINANCE: THE VIRTUE OF FINDING VALUE IN PURPOSE

Up until now, we have touched on two macro objectives:

1. The survival of your business (defense) and
2. Engineering your business's rise to market dominance (offense).

As discussed in Chapter 1, in both instances, *adaptability* is the core principle upon which every change that will guide your business along its journey of necessary transformation is founded. If survival is your only macro objective, you don't need to worry about adding *innovation* and *disruption* to your to-do list. If, however, survival isn't good enough, go ahead and add those two mechanisms to your list of imperatives.

Your list should now look like this:

• Adaptability
• Innovation
• Disruption

The 3 indispensable traits of organizations in regards to digital transformation.

Fig. 3.1: **Adaption, Innovation, Disruption**

Simple enough. Now let's take things a little further. As we just discussed, the *experience economy* isn't just a huge, confusing change. It also provide adaptable businesses with abundant new opportunities, all of which are connected by a single and common thread. This thread can be summed up in a single question:

• How can we create better, more remarkable experiences for our customers?

By combining this question and our three imperatives, we can start to give direction to our budding digital transformation initiative.

• **Adaptability** - How can we adapt to create better experiences for our customers?
• **Innovation** - How can innovation help us create better experiences for our customers?

- **Disruption** - How can we disrupt our market to deliver better experiences for our customers?

These questions may seem simple, but most businesses fail to go through this process entirely or fail to follow through with it. One of the primary reasons they don't follow through is that they forget to connect these types of initiatives to any kind of timeline. Thus, they only exist as ideas, as abstractions. They never make the jump from *idea* to *deliverable*.

TAKING THE FIRST STEP: MAKING THE JUMP FROM IDEA TO DELIVERABLE

To help you avoid the inertia that keeps most businesses from turning game-changing *ideas* into *actions*, let's ask three simple, critical questions that every business should ask regularly.

1. What can we fix?
2. What can we improve?
3. How can we disrupt our industry?

WHAT CAN
WE FIX?

WHAT CAN
WE IMPROVE?

HOW CAN WE
DISPRUPT?

Fig. 3.2: **Fixing, Improving, Disrupting**

Simple enough, right? And yet, there is a piece missing. Can you spot it?

Now let's add a little utility and momentum to these questions by connecting them to the real world — the world of getting things done rather than just making wish lists.

1. What can we fix *today*?
2. What can we improve *this quarter*?
3. How can we disrupt our industry *this year*?

WHAT CAN
WE FIX
TODAY?

WHAT CAN
WE IMPROVE
THIS QUARTER?

HOW CAN WE DISRUPT
OUR INDUSTRY
THIS YEAR?

Fig. 3.3: **Fixing, Improving, Disrupting**

By making these simple changes, we accomplished two crucial goals. First, we have begun to set a timeline for completion of every item on our list. *Fixes* are short-term. *Improvements* are short- to mid-term. *Disruption* is long term, but not so long as to be out of reach. Second, we have begun to teach our organization how to *organize* and *prioritize* its natural transformation lifecycles. We have mapped them out. This is important because understanding how to manage and schedule small, medium and large changes makes *change management* a lot simpler.

Once everyone in the organization understands that *fixes* are identified and addressed daily, the organization becomes tasked with making sure everything is working as it should. If this feels like a *broken window* policy (if you see a broken window in your building, fix it immediately instead of putting off until later), you aren't wrong. Is there a typo on the website? Don't wait until another 20,000 visitors have spotted it before fixing it. Do it right away. Is your app or shopping cart glitchy? Don't wait until 800 customers have given up on buying your product to notice or do something about it. *Fix* problems *immediately*.

The hierarchy is simple — fixes first, improvements second and disruption third. This isn't to say that disruption is less important than improvements. The hierarchy refers to urgency only, not value.

Sometimes, flawless execution in itself is disruptive. Have you ever heard someone say they really like a certain website, product or service because "it just works?" The little things, when done perfectly, can be quite disruptive.

THE IMPORTANCE OF CREATING A PRIORITY STRUCTURE FOR ANY KIND OF CHANGE MANAGEMENT OR TRANSFORMATION PROJECT.

Prioritizing the scheduling of deliverables by *category* (fixes first, improvements second and disruption third) creates a *predictable structure* around the scheduling of an organization's transformation. It may seem like a detail, but this is actually a huge deal.

One of the most common causes of frustration, stress, friction, and failure in *every* transformation project is *confusion*. Managers make the mistake of treating *every* change or task as *high priority* or *no particular priority*. This is an efficiency killer, a morale killer and, ultimately, a project killer.

Repeat this: *If everything is urgent, nothing is urgent.*

Project managers who don't take the time to separate urgent tasks from not-so-urgent tasks end up overwhelming and confusing their staffs.

Likewise, project managers who don't take the time to map out and communicate the entire lifecycle of their projects end up overwhelming and confusing their staffs.

The type of *prioritization* and context we are talking about with fixes, improvements and disruption will create *clarity* and *predictability* in your organization's transformation, which will result in less stress, less friction, fewer mistakes, and much smoother progress.

HOW DOES THIS ALL FIT TOGETHER?

Let's connect the dots between both sets of questions:

1. **Adaptability:** How can we adapt to create better experiences for our customers?

- What customer experiences can we *fix* today?
- What customer experiences can we *improve* this quarter?
- What customer experiences can we *significantly improve* this year?

2. **Innovation:** How can innovation help us create better experiences for our customers?
   - What customer experiences can innovation help us improve *this quarter*?
   - What customer experiences can innovation help us improve *this year*?
   - What innovations might help us improve key customer experiences next year?

3. **Disruption:** How can we disrupt our market to deliver better experiences for our customers?
   - How should we disrupt our industry *this year*?
   - How should we plan to disrupt our industry *next year*?
   - What types of customer experiences should be at the heart of our milestones of disruption?
   - What types of innovation might help us accomplish these goals?

See how that all plugs in nicely?

When we talk about *innovation*, we are not just talking about technology (software and hardware). Look to services, infrastructure, channels, business methodologies, logistics, psychology, medicine, sociology, pop culture, economics, etc. Cast as broad a net as possible when considering what to innovate.

Always make a point to look for ideas *outside* of your industry. Today's most innovative companies base their success on their ability to find solutions to problems in industries and sectors not previously connected to theirs. Real innovative genius is not linear. More often than not, it lies in being able to merge two (or more) disconnected ideas into something entirely new and useful.

As an example, many of us compare our business relationships to our best customer experiences across any industry. Perhaps you love how the barista at Starbucks knows your name, your kids' names and your favorite drink. This makes you wonder why one of your suppliers takes three days to call you back. The great experience with your barista becomes a benchmark for other experiences you want to have. Many companies miss this entirely by only looking within their own industry.

BUT WHAT ABOUT MY OTHER BUSINESS OBJECTIVES? HOW DO THEY FIT IN ALL OF THIS?

A few pages ago, we explained binary business motivators like *survival* and *dominance*, then moved on to rudimentary objectives (*adaptation, improvement and disruption*), then used what we learned to create the foundations of an actionable *transformative* business strategy. Not a bad start. Now let's take a look at how typical business objectives fit in.

If you are a CEO or a business manager, your basic list of macro objectives probably looks a little like this:

- Increase revenue,
- Attract more customers and
- Improve profitability.

If you prefer targets over objectives, your list might look a little more like this:

- +15% year over year (YOY) revenue,
- +10,000 net new customers and
- Improve margins by 1.3%.

Depending on how involved your business plan is or how involved you are in the details of it, your list of objectives might include some of the following:

- Increase customer *buy rate* (purchasing frequency),
- Reduce customer *erosion* (customers no longer being customers),
- Increase average *yield* (the value of each transaction),
- acquire more actionable data from customers,
- Increase positive reviews and social recommendations,
- Improve advertising effectiveness,
- Improve loyalty (longer customer lifecycles),
- Acquire more social media followers,
- Drive more traffic to various digital properties,
- Improve the quality and stickiness of our content,
- Drive more app downloads,
- Increase time spent in our stores (digital or brick-and-mortar),
- Improve customer service, and/or
- Improve our checkout experience.

Any of these look familiar? If the answer is yes, you are off to a good start. If the answer is no, you might have some work to do to identify and list your business objectives before we go on. (Don't forget to add a section about *improving customer experiences* if you haven't already.)

Assuming that the answer to our last question was yes, we have some good news. Digital transformation is going to help you address all of these objectives more effectively than you are. How? By ensuring that every aspect of your digital transformation plugs into these objectives.

In addition to finding ways of adapting, innovating and disrupting to create better experiences for your customers, you also will do the same for these goals.

Once your company settles into its ability to adapt to new market paradigms, you begin questioning how to use innovation and disruption to:

- Increase customer *buy rate* (purchasing frequency),
- Reduce customer *erosion* (customers no longer being customers),
- Increase average *yield* (the value of each transaction),
- Acquire more actionable data from customers,
- Increase positive reviews and social recommendations,
- Improve advertising effectiveness,
- Improve loyalty (longer customer lifecycles),
- Acquire more social media followers,
- Drive more traffic to various digital properties,
- Improve the quality and stickiness of our content,
- Drive more app downloads,
- Increase time spent in our stores (digital or brick-and-mortar),
- Improve customer service,
- Improve our checkout experience, and anything else you can measure in your business.

Next, how can innovation and disruption be used to:

- Deliver the most remarkable customer experiences in our industry,
- Completely redefine our category,
- Own our category inside of three years, and
- Make our competitors obsolete inside of five years?

We've all heard that *the best defense is a good offense*, but it doesn't hurt to be reminded of it and to be shown exactly how. It isn't just a saying. It's real. It's at the core of every company's *success* and every successful company's *longevity*. It's what makes the difference between Netflix and Blockbuster, Apple and Blackberry, and Amazon and Circuit City. The success plus longevity math in your industry is no different. It's the same everywhere.

You already have an advantage over your competitors. You're reading this book. Three chapters in, you already know more about building dragons, business Darwinism, the massive opportunity that is the experience economy, and how to customize a digital transformation journey to fit your company's real-world business objectives. Not a bad way to start, and there's plenty more on the way.

We're going to change gears a bit and discuss how to incorporate customer experience design into any business, but we *will* return to our discussion about business objectives later in the book. We just need to cover a few other topics first.

CHAPTER 4:

AN EXPERIENCE-FOCUSED APPROACH TO CUSTOMER AND EMPLOYEE ENGAGEMENT

Everything a business does is ultimately about creating and delivering experiences — product design, retail design, website design, customer service, and so on. Every customer-facing detail of your business is a *user experience* (UX) project. Companies that realize this early and work to capitalize on this vital piece of insight usually manage to grow into what marketing experts call *lovebrands*. *Lovebrands* are brands that the majority of the public tends to admire, whether they are customers of these brands or not. Notable examples are Apple, Zappos, BMW, and Starbucks.

It isn't to say that these brands don't have their tribes of devoted trolls and detractors, but they *do* generally land at the top of most consumers' and industry analysts' lists when asked what brands they admire the most.

What is interesting about *lovebrands* is that, while the most successful among them are known for their UX prowess in regard to customer touchpoints, they also owe much of their success to another key aspect of the experience design equation — *internal* experience design. This internal dimension of UX design focuses almost exclusively on employee touchpoints and employee experience design. Although often ignored, this aspect of UX is as vital to a company's success as its more visible *external* counterpart.

It is important then, whenever we talk about UX and experience design, to look at both market-facing UX and experience design, and employee-facing UX and experience design.

The value of internal experience design can be illustrated thus:

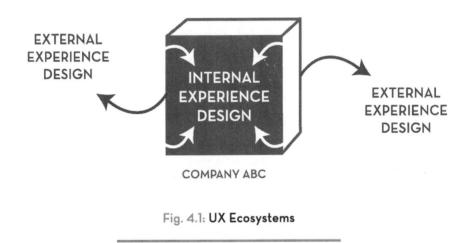

Fig. 4.1: **UX Ecosystems**

EXPERIENCE DESIGN AND COMPANY CULTURE

When business analysts talk about a *company culture* they are referencing a living, breathing, self-supporting social and operational ecosystem built on a specific framework of employee touchpoints. They aren't just talking about a general mood or an abstract way of doing things.

For instance:

- Every interaction between employees and managers is a touchpoint,
- Every interaction between employees and the tools they use (from a piece of software to the type of computer they use) is a touchpoint,
- Every internal rule and procedure is a touchpoint,
- The tone and content of every internal email is a touchpoint,
- Every workspace and meeting room is a touchpoint,
- The frequency and value of every meeting employees are scheduled to attend are touchpoints, and
- Everything from the first handshake during the hiring process

to the way employees are treated at the end of their tenure at a company is a touchpoint.

Every touchpoint creates an experience. As these touchpoints become part of every employee's daily life, the experiences they create start to form a whole. That whole, over time, becomes cumulatively positive or negative.

Just like with customers, a preponderance of negative or less-than-stellar experiences in the workplace tend to fuel disappointment, apathy, cynicism, and a progressive state of disengagement, which negatively affects morale, productivity and engagement. The flip side of that equation is that a preponderance of positive and stellar experiences in the workplace tend to drive excitement, engagement, morale, productivity, and even loyalty.

ANNUAL COST OF UNHAPPY EMPLOYEES TO US COMPANIES.
(Source: Gallup-Healthways Well-Being Index.)
Productivity, missed days, employee erosion, etc

DEGREE TO WHICH COMPANIES WITH AN ENGAGED WORKFORCE OUTPERFORM COMPANIES WITH A DISENGAGED WORKFORCE.
(Source: Engaging Employees: What Drives Employee Engagement and Why It Matters, Dale Carnegie Institute.)

THE AVERAGE INCREASE IN SALES FOR COMPANIES WHOSE EMPLOYEES ARE ENGAGED COMPARED TO COMPANIES WHOSE EMPLOYEES ARE NOT ENGAGED.
(Source: Shawn Achor, Positive Intelligence, Harvard Business Review.)

HOW MUCH MORE PRODUCTIVE HAPPY EMPLOYEES ARE COMPARED TO UNHAPPY EMPLOYEES.
(Source: Happiness and Productivity, University of Warwick.)

HOW MUCH MORE CREATIVE HAPPY EMPLOYEES ARE COMPARED TO UNHAPPY EMPLOYEES.
(Source: Sonja Lyubomirsky, Laura King, and Ed Diener, Positive Intelligence, Harvard Business Review.)
Since adaptation and innovation depend on creativity, this is important.

Fig. 4.2: **How Employees Impact the Brand Experience**

Organizations that understand the power and value of designing positive experiences understand that experience *design* is not an exercise in experience *chance*. It is born out of a *deliberate* effort to create *positive* and ideally *delightful* experiences. This means that employee-facing company cultures, just like customer-facing brand cultures, cannot be left to chance. They have to be *designed, managed, measured,* and *improved* at every opportunity. This requires a deliberate *focus* and a dedicated internal *practice*.

EXPERIENCE DESIGN AND ENGAGEMENT

Emotions and attitudes are contagious. Someone with a bad attitude tends to bring every down. Likewise, someone with a positive attitude tends to cheer everyone up. Attitudes and moods *are* contagious.

Business environments also are social environments, meaning positive and negative attitudes can spread like viruses across offices, departments and even large, regional business units. It is vital to ensure that the attitudes that spread across an organization are the kind that will drive and reinforce *positive* experiences rather than negative ones. Here's why:

As a consumer, think about how you feel when you walk into a store whose employees are upbeat, eager to help and obviously happy to be there. Now think about how you feel when you walk into a store where the employees are stressed, unpleasant and obviously not thrilled to be there. Which store will you be most likely to shop in again? Which store are you most likely to recommend to your family and friends? Which store are you most likely to spend more money in? This phenomenon isn't limited to retail or B2C, by the way. It also extends to B2B.

Engagement is a product *and* a source of positive or negative experiences. It is a cog in the experience design wheel. Whether it turns out to be an effective cog or a dysfunctional one depends on the type of company culture you create. It also depends on the extent to which your organization designs every possible experience, including internal ones, to create a continuum of positive experiences.

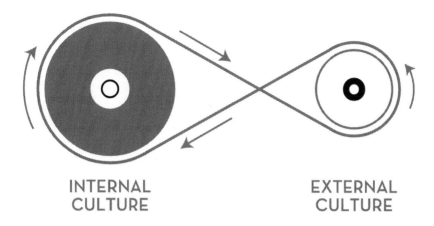

INTERNAL
CULTURE

EXTERNAL
CULTURE

Fig. 4.3: Internal Culture and External Culture

BRINGING IT ALL TOGETHER

Internally, one of the principal objectives of organizational experience design should be to *drive employee engagement*. But what does employee engagement look like? How is it gauged? Consider parameters such as employees' eagerness to:

- Contribute to coworkers' and peers' success,
- Contribute to overall company success (macro),
- Contribute to a particular project's success (micro),
- Contribute to positive customer experiences,
- Contribute positively to overall morale,
- Eagerness to recruit talent to join the company,
- Eagerness to help recruit new customers, clients and partners, and
- Eagerness to be more productive.

The list can be shortened or lengthened as needed, but the basics of positive engagement are there. They consist of an eagerness to contribute to the business in positive ways. Building a culture of employee engagement drives positive outcomes. Any employee experience that doesn't drive one or more of these outcomes needs to be evaluated and either improved or eliminated.

To further illustrate why this is so important, these positive outcomes tend to manifest themselves as the following:

- Increased productivity,
- Increased employee loyalty,
- Improved talent retention,
- Improved customer satisfaction,
- Increased customer loyalty,
- More customer referrals,
- More repeat business,
- Improved company reputation, and
- Access to a larger share of the industry's best talent.

It may seem counterintuitive to focus on internal engagement when so much of the recent "engagement" conversation has been about customer engagement, but engaged employees create engaged customers.

Engaged employees create engaged customers. You don't have to print it on a T-shirt (in fact, don't), but it's worth remembering. Before a company can build a successful customer engagement practice, it has to start by building a culture of employee engagement. A companywide engaged culture is an essential and unavoidable foundation. This is something that too many companies have lost sight of. Fortunately, *lovebrands* and some of today's most successful companies are living case studies of the power of employee engagement design.

Externally, the process is essentially the same. Instead of creating positive experiences for employees to drive employee engagement, create positive experiences for customers to drive customer engagement. What does customer engagement look like? How is it gauged? It includes an eagerness to:

- Tie their own identity to the company or brand,
- Contribute to the brand's success and growth (macro),
- Contribute to a product's success and adoption (micro),
- Eagerness to share their positive experiences with others,
- Eagerness to help others discover the brand, a product, or an experience,
- Eagerness to interact with the company on social and other channels,
- Eagerness to help share company's content, and
- Eagerness to grow relationship with the brand (mindshare and/or walletshare).

Any customer experience that doesn't drive at least one of these outcomes is either useless or detrimental to the company's journey toward market dominance. This was true in the pre-digital age, when recommendations and word-of-mouth were limited to the water cooler and small spheres of influence. It is even truer today, in an age where a single recommendation or customer review can not only make or break a reputation, but affect the success of a product launch, influence millions of potential customers, and even impact a company's stock price.

If you are starting to understand the internal/external experience design continuum and how engaged employees driving engaged customers subsequently drives growth, profitability and success, good. We haven't talked about products or services in this chapter. We have discussed how to leverage experience design (internally and externally) as a platform through which to encourage specific types of engagement that drive positive business outcomes. None of this is particularly revolutionary, but look around. How many companies actually operate this way? How many companies actively build experience design into their operations? Among them, how many use experience design to drive engagement? And among those, how many use engagement to effectively drive specific business outcomes? Speaking of business outcomes of engagement, here is a short list.

Revenue focused business outcomes include increased:

- Customer retention (longer customer lifecycles),
- Customer spend per transaction (short term),
- Buy rates (short *and* long term), and
- Customer lifetime value (long term).

Market-growth focused business outcomes include:

- Improved brand and product discovery,
- Increased brand and product mindshare,
- More customer referrals,
- Improved brand image, and
- Increased brand loyalty.

As with its earlier internal counterpart, this list of outcomes can be lengthened or shortened as needed, but it is a good start. Who wouldn't want to increase customer retention, customer-spend and customer referrals, right? These types of outcomes can and should be (at least in part) driven by specific types of engagement, and these types of engagement should be part of a properly designed customer experience strategy.

By this point, most of the dots should feel fairly well connected. Now let's talk about one last thing before we move on to the next piece of the digital transformation puzzle.

WHY ARE WE NOT DISCUSSING TECHNOLOGY YET?

Technology obviously plays a big part in successful digital transformation. But, for the time being, let's not think about any specific technologies like collaboration software, Customer Relationship Management (CRM) solutions, cloud, or big data. For now, it is more important that you think of process, experience design and outcomes. Understanding what specific problems you want to solve and what types of experiences you want to create, internally and externally, will inform your choice of tools and solutions, not the other way around.

Starting with pain points, the groundwork that comes first involves the following:

1. Identifying every pain point related to your company, internally and externally,
2. Understanding the impact these pain points have on your company's internal and external ecosystems,
3. Identifying who in your company's universe of employees, partners and customers, is best suited to make these pain points disappear and replace them with positive, remarkable, exceptional experiences,
4. Prioritizing these pain points to ensure that the most crucial ones are tackled first,
5. Providing the individuals and teams tasked with these redesign projects with the authority and resources to succeed,
6. Testing and evaluating the improvements (essentially looking for new or lingering pain points), and
7. Repeating this process as many times as necessary.

While pain points are always a great place to start, the other half of this process is a little more creative and forward looking, as it involves looking for ways of improving experiences where no pain points may yet exist (or at least are not yet obvious). For this, remember our earlier hockey quote about not skating where the puck is, but rather where the puck will be. Here is how that translates in regard to our current discussion. Because technology changes so fast, and today's most competitive companies innovate around improving utility, functionality and experiences fast and hard, the enemy of competitiveness is, as ever, complacency.

At this juncture, it is vital to understand that today's positive experience for a customer or employee already is becoming tomorrow's pain point. (Think about how miraculous 2008 CRM software seemed in 2008. Now imagine if you were *still* using that exact same software today.) This means that executives and digital transformation agents have to constantly and proactively look for opportunities to improve today's positive experiences, while simultaneously replacing existing pain points with remarkable experiences. The notion of *continuous improvement* isn't new, but, as technology continues to advance faster than ever before, a focus on continuous improvement is more important than it has been in the past. More to the point, continuous improvement must be applied specifically to experience design, not just traditional areas like productivity and logistics. If your company is not working to build an organization-wide focus on experience design innovation, it always will be second to companies that do.

SUMMARY

1. Your company's two main areas of focus when it comes to experience design should be:

   1. Eliminating pain points. (Turning negative experiences into positive ones.)
   2. Looking for ways to improve positive experiences. (Driving experience design innovation.)

2. Rather than focusing almost exclusively on external (customer-facing) experience design, your company should focus equally on internal (employee-facing) experience design.

CHAPTER 5:

PEOPLE'S NEEDS, NOT TECHNOLOGY, ARE AT THE CORE OF DIGITAL TRANSFORMATION

We just discussed the importance of experience design in employee and customer engagement, the importance of using engagement to drive key business outcomes and build a competitive advantage, and how this process should guide a company's technology adoption and digital transformation. Now, let's talk about the most important consideration of all (Yes, even more important than technology.) — people.

FROM PEOPLE TO NUMBERS AND BACK TO PEOPLE AGAIN

By now, you have most likely heard of the *H2H* movement. If not, *H2H* is an abbreviation for *human-to-human*. The principle is simple: Forget about B2C and B2B. Business really is all *H2H* — human-to-human. In other words, business is about people. It's about relationships: Humanize your business or die.

As formulaic and facile as this sort of business insight may seem, it's correct. From the beginning of time, commerce always has been about people and relationships. We *naturally* want to do business with people we like, people we know and people we trust. There is *always* a social, human component to a business relationship. Humans have an innate need to form bonds. Businesses that capitalize on that core human element have an advantage over businesses that choose to focus mostly on securing the next transaction. (Nobody likes to just be a number, right? Nobody likes being marketed to. Both *human connection* and a *validation of our value as people* have to figure into *every* relationship we have with the companies we do business with. It doesn't matter if it is a shoe retailer or a bank.)

A company's understanding of the value of people as *people*, not just as nameless, faceless customers and employees, lies at the core of what we are discussing. Customers and employees are not randomly interchangeable items on a spreadsheet. They are not drones or numbers or *headcounts*. Each brings a unique set of insights, capacity and tangential value that extends far beyond the kernel of their primary and more obvious purpose (as either *transaction actors* or *headcount*). *Identifying* that unique value package then *leveraging* it is what separates high growth business from every other *also-in* competitor.

The problem facing the business world today is that decades of conditioning and limited access to data and agile computing power have taught us to do the exact opposite. Between interactions, customers are still, more often than not, treated as nameless, faceless numbers on spreadsheets. Improvements in technology have allowed most companies to look at their customer data by gender, age, location, and behaviors, but a) segmentation is still mostly rigid and formulaic, and b) customer data isn't as granular as it could be. These limitations are disappearing, and you need to prepare for the opportunity this creates for your business.

"THE CUSTOMER IS KING" (TCIK) WAS ONLY THE BEGINNING

Everyone understands the inherent value of the phrase "the customer is king." In a perfect world, every customer would walk away from their most recent experience with your company feeling like royalty, delighted by their purchase, awed by the perfect service they received, and eager to repeat the experience and/or share it.

If you only gauge customer experiences by three criteria, on a scale of 1-5, with 1 being "not at all" and 5 being "extremely," here is a good place to start:

1. How delighted were you by your purchase or experience?
2. How amazed were you by the quality of our service?
3. How eager are you to share it with friends and loved ones?

Remember the conversation we had about focusing on areas of improvement in Chapter 4? These three questions play into that effort. Keep pushing for a perfect score on those three questions, and you will be on the right track.

Unfortunately, making customers feel *that* good about every interaction is exceedingly difficult and expensive. The logistics and resources required to pull off a uniform and consistent TCIK strategy eludes most businesses, especially once they have reached a certain size. (Why size is relevant is a point we will return to.) Up until a few years ago, only three categories of businesses consistently did TCIK right — luxury brands, boutique businesses and mid-to-high-level service industry brands.

Why size matters is simple: One of the secret ingredients of a successful TCIK strategy is personalization. By *personalization*, we don't mean monogrammed shirts and letterhead. Personalization refers to a business's ability to give a customer the impression that he or she is *known, special* and *appreciated* as an individual, not just another customer. This isn't about *customer* service, it's about *personal* service. Everyone the customer interacts with knows his or her name, preferences, and history. There is a familiarity in this model that denotes interest, affection and respect from the business. Being greeted by name and having staff remember you dives deeper into the meaning of *value* than the effective uniformity of even the best traditional "customer service" model.

If "just being a number" stands at one end of the TCIK spectrum, a company representative greeting you as if you are their most appreciated and missed customer stands at the opposite end. On a scale of 1-5, with 5 being the highest possible score, building effective personalization into every interaction a customer has with a company scores a solid 5 every time.

We previously mentioned that the size of an organization impacts its ability to deliver this level of customer interaction. This is because human-to-human, the sort of personalization we are talking about, comes down to customers' and employees' ability to build and maintain relationships over time.

First, the more customers a business has, the more difficult it is for employees (human touchpoints) to remember who these customers are and build relationships with them. There are actual limitations to how many relationships human beings can have. It is generally accepted that human beings, on average, can maintain about 150 engaged social relationships at any given time. These are relationships in which a subject is able to recognize another individual and understand how they fit into his or her world. This number is commonly referred to as *Dunbar's Number* (named after anthropologist Robert Dunbar, who first suggested it). [27] This limitation is theorized to be the result of our brains' limited neocortical processing capacity. It is important to note that the number is an average, and that the range probably falls more between 100 and 300. The point is that our capacity to form engaged bonds with others is biologically limited. This has a huge impact on a business's ability to create genuine personalized experiences for customers at scale.

Second, the more employees a company has, the less likely it is that customers will interact with the same employee every time, which means that the relationship and personalization piece of the ideal customer experience model cannot scale. The customer might get great customer service every time, but it won't be truly personalized.

Third, the more people a company hires the more likely it is that a certain percentage of them won't have the qualities necessary to build lasting relationships with customers or meet the exacting criteria that luxury brands, boutique businesses, and mid-to-high-end service industry brands are known for.

Think back to some of your favorite experiences with businesses. Think about the favorite people you have dealt with. Maybe it's your barber or hairdresser. Maybe it's your neighborhood butcher who always asks about how your kids are doing in school, or that barista who remembers how you like your coffee before you even have to ask. It could be your go-to shoe expert at your favorite running store or your favorite waiter, or the one accounts receivable person you know will always put you at the top of the pile and go the extra mile to take care of you. For the reasons listed above, it has traditionally been very hard to scale that. A point that you can expect to keep coming up in this book however, is that problem = opportunity: If personalized experiences have tremendous value, and every business of a certain size has trouble creating personalized experiences, it stands to reason that the few businesses who figure out how to scale personalized experiences will enjoy a tremendous advantage over the competition.

---

[27]Dunbar, R. I. (2010). *How many friends does one person need?: Dunbar's number and other evolutionary quirks.* Cambridge, MA: Harvard University Press.

In the age of experience, this is one of the principal challenges facing companies… and, therefore, one of the greatest opportunities for companies to gain a significant market advantage over their less *aware* and adaptable competitors.

You're also in luck, because technology can help you do just that, and that is a topic what we are now going to explore.

TCIK AND THE EXPERIENCE ECONOMY: BUILDING A FOUNDATION FOR WHAT COMES NEXT

There is one company that puts experience design at the heart of everything it does and somehow manages to scale it better than any other — Disney.

Walt Disney was obsessed with creating magical experiences for Disneyland visitors. "Magical" isn't just a buzzword here. Walt was serious about creating magical experiences for every single guest of his parks. Experience design was at the core of everything he built. He understood the importance of what we now refer to as the *experience economy* and worked tirelessly to build an entire business around it. It wasn't an add-on. It was a core principle, a foundation, a purpose. That takes care of the vision and commitment piece of the equation. Now let's talk about execution.

Two key principles guided Walt Disney's people-centric approach to experience design thinking. They are as valid today as they were then:

1. Optimize the mundane. This means taking nothing for granted and recognizing that every experience is important; every detail matters, no matter how insignificant it may seem.

For example, the output of the ambient sound systems in Disney parks is calibrated to be roughly the same, no matter where you are in the park. This is a spectacular achievement, given the degree of technical complexity it requires. It may seem obsessive and silly, as no park guest would consciously notice decibel inconsistencies across the park, but every optimized bit of experience is a link in a much larger chain.

Similarly, the placement of garbage bins in Disney parks is optimized to within an inch of perfection because even the distance between a food vendor and a garbage bin can be optimized to reduce littering.

Too close, and a guest may not be ready to throw away their napkins and wrapper yet. Too far, and that guest might have already discarded of trash in a less than ideal way. If litter is a pain point, this is its most effective solution.

Optimizing the mundane isn't a radical idea. It's a foundational one.

We aren't even talking about personalization yet, or the sweet, glossy aspect of creating magical experiences. These two examples are about as unsexy and unnoticeable as it gets. And yet, they're the foundation upon which the cool stuff is built. The lesson here is, if you get the basics wrong, if you cut corners to focus on the sexier aspects of experience design, you will never achieve excellence. Take a page from Walt's experience economy playbook and remember to optimize the mundane. Most companies out there, even those that pride themselves on providing outstanding customer experiences, often forget to do this. Don't make the same mistake.

2. Build your company around *shared purpose*. If you tell your employees that their purpose is to help the company "maximize shareholder value," you aren't playing in the experience economy. You aren't even playing in the customer service economy. It may be a legitimate objective, but that can't be its employees' shared purpose. For example, Disney focuses on keeping the magic of childhood alive. That's its shared purpose. Consider the impact this has on customer-facing employees. Now imagine how different Disney parks would be if the shared purpose were "maximizing shareholder value" instead.

We wrote earlier about the importance of properly and clearly articulating the company's vision. This is an extension of that. Your organization is made up of people. People tend to naturally rally around missions and purpose that they understand and believe in. They are far more likely to work toward a *meaningful* shared purpose that actually has value for them and your customers than one which rewards the company and investors, but has little relevance to their daily work. For many companies, this may require a radical cultural shift, but that's okay. It is a necessary one. You can still aim to maximize shareholder value and profits. You just *also* need to incorporate a people-centric focus — one that regards customers and employees as *experience shareholders* — and build a *shared purpose* strategy to drive this critical dimension of your business.

DIGITAL TRANSFORMATION AND TECHNOLOGY'S IMPACT ON SCALING TCIK

Fast forward to today's Disney Parks experience and you will notice the degree to which technology and experience design are intertwined. We aren't talking about animatronics pirates and space mission simulations. We are talking about the holy grail of experience design — people-centric personalization so seamless and natural that it almost seems magical. How does Disney do it?

The company has invested in technology solutions that *enable* its two core principles: 1) optimizing the mundane and 2) realizing their shared value (which, in their case, focuses on creating magical experiences). As Arthur C. Clarke once said, "any sufficiently advanced technology is indistinguishable from magic. [28]" The folks at Disney seem to have taken Clarke's words to heart, and it paid off.

If you aren't familiar with Disney's MagicBand technology, here is your quick tour. The MagicBand is a stylish looking rubberized bracelet equipped with an RFID chip, a small radio and a battery. Disney park visitors either receive their own personalized MagicBand in the mail shortly after booking their visit or pick it up when they arrive. Once on their wrist, the bands connect them to tens of thousands of strategically located sensors and beacons around the park and its properties. On the surface, the bracelet serves as a wallet, key, ticket, and ID, which is pretty convenient, but the tech does much more than that. The second and slightly deeper layer of experience design these bracelets help create is a frictionless experience for guests. As the park tracks the bracelets and analyzes individual visitor data (age, preferences, hotel, etc.), the park adapts to its visitors' needs. Frictionless experiences mean not having to wait in endless lines anymore or figure out what shuttle to take from point A to point B. It means painless hotel check-ins and checkouts. It takes the guessing out of what to do next, which frees visitors to take advantage of more rides while they are there.

The third layer is where the real magic happens. Wherever you go, your bracelet sends a signal to a nearby sensor that you are there. This information is transmitted to likely human touchpoints in the vicinity with whom you will probably interact. So, when you arrive at a restaurant, for example, the host will not ask you the usual introductory questions. He or she will know who you are before you even make eye contact with them. They will know how many people are in your party. If you have pre-ordered your food, your wait time will be minimal as sensors throughout the park have predicted your arrival time and sent the order

---

[28]Clarke, A. C. (1962). *Profiles of the future; an inquiry into the limits of the possible.* New York: Harper & Row.

accordingly. If you have not, menu items might be proposed first based on your preferences, which already have been crunched by the park's computers. More magical still, your food will find you, regardless of where you decide to sit. Though no one in the park has ever met you or developed a relationship with you, it will seem as if everyone knows you, appreciates you and anticipates your needs as if they had known you for years. (Done properly, this is extraordinary rather than creepy.) Remember our earlier discussion about the biological limitation known as *Dunbar's Number* and how personalized interactions are difficult to scale? This is an example of technology elegantly solving (or at least bypassing) a problem that was insurmountable a decade ago.

If you have worked even as little as a day in customer service or client support, you already know that this is CRM evolved to a science-fiction-like degree of performance. Except that it isn't science fiction anymore. It's real. Disney is using it. Chances are your company isn't using it yet, but it could be. Whether you are a big box retailer, a small restaurant chain, a specialty manufacturer, or an insurance provider, you can implement this clever application of data collection, cloud computing and a touch of AI. That's it. You no longer have to invest billions into a complex IT infrastructure if you don't want to.

THAT'S ALL FINE AND GOOD, BUT HOW DOES THIS HELP MY BUSINESS?

A few observations that bring us back to our original dragon-building discussion:

1. Disney's technological integration and innovative thinking is as brilliant as it gets, but if you take a step back and look at the basic building blocks of its digital transformation over time, all Disney really did was cleverly combine ubiquitous technologies to drive its core objectives and optimize its desired outcomes.

Rule No. 1: Disney kept its eye on the ball and didn't deviate from it or try to reinvent itself. Creating the most magical and personalized experiences possible was always the end game.

Rule No. 2: Disney applied its technological evolution, its digital transformation, to its stated goals and mission. Its digital transformation had purpose. It wasn't just an *also-in*, one-size-fits-all template. It is almost an all-size-fits-one approach, representing what personalization can feel like when done well.

Stick to those two rules, and you won't lose your way.

2. Disney didn't fall into the usual digital transformation trap of focusing on superficial projects that sound "digital" but have limited impact on the company's value. Its transformation wasn't about integrating social media and *digital* content into its marketing communications, for example. It went further, much further. It understood that its digital transformation and technological innovation had to be rooted in its core principles and purpose. Disney approached the experience economy as a massive opportunity that transcended its products and services while helping boost their value. In this particular instance, it shed its own skin and this aspect of its business emerged a newer, stronger, better version of itself.

3. Any company can replicate what Disney accomplished. We don't mean the RFID bracelets and sensors bit. Disney's choice to leverage this particular technology is informed by their specific business model. (Retailers can't expect customers to wear RFID bracelets, for instance, and the B2B world even less so. Resort hotels certainly can, however, and hospitals and schools, not to mention the potential for tourism applications, but I digress.) That particular piece of the tech puzzle isn't going to work for everyone, but the other pieces will: Big data, cloud computing, AI (artificial intelligence), and connected devices, – usually referred to as IoT (the *Internet of Things*). All of these technologies and more can be combined to create an infinite number of unique and customized people-centric solutions whose purpose, within the context of the experience economy, is to:

• Eradicate pain points,
• Optimize the mundane,
• Personalize interactions, and
• Create magical (remarkable) experiences.

How your company decides to combine these technologies to accomplish these and other objectives is entirely up to you. Retailers are already using wifi beacons and mobile technology to create better experiences for their customers, and municipalities are using sensors and cameras to create better experiences for their residents and visitors. What matters is that you understand that the toolkit is there, the toolkit is infinitely adaptable and companies that invest adequate time and effort into using technology to build people-centric business processes that are rooted in experience design tend to be first in line to reap the benefits of that investment. Examples of companies that have done this include: Amazon, Zappos, Netflix, Apple, Starbucks, Virgin America, Google, and even Microsoft.

Let's play a little game to put this all in perspective.

Imagine you were hired by an airline. How would you combine IoT (Internet of Things), mobile, cloud, big data, and AI to identify and eradicate traveler pain points? (ROI translation: Reduce customer erosion, increase customer loyalty and grow customer lifetime value.)

What if a hotel chain or a shopping mall hired you? How might you use IoT, mobile, cloud, big data, and AI to personalize interactions and create magical experiences for your guests? (ROI translation: Improve customer loyalty and referrals, increase digital and foot traffic, increase average customer-spend, and grow customer lifetime value.)

Now imagine that an online retailer or service provider hired you. How would you combine these technologies to help them optimize the mundane? (ROI translation: Increase average customer spend, drive more repeat business and increase buy rate.)

Take your time. Grab something to write or sketch with, and work through any or all of these hypotheticals. By the time you're done, you should begin to see how all the pieces fit.

THE OTHER HALF OF THE PEOPLE-CENTRIC EQUATION: EMPLOYEES

While we have spent most of this chapter focused on customer experiences and principles of TCIK, the technologies we are discussing also can be used to:

- Eradicate internal pain points,
- Optimize the mundane in the workplace,
- Personalize collaboration, and
- Help drive employee engagement.

At its most passive, building a people-centric business that empowers employees to easily create outstanding experiences for customers helps create a positive and rewarding culture of employee engagement. With a little bit of deliberate focus, the right combination of technologies and processes can become a platform for in-house innovation, tremendous productivity and accelerated progress.

While it was crucial to focus on the importance of creating outward-facing people-centric experiences, don't forget that there is an internal component to this as well. We will revisit it later in the book, but, for now, make a mental note that all of the principles outlined in this chapter can be applied equally to customers and employees. Establishing a balance between your company's inner and outer worlds will help make all of its moving parts work well together.

CHAPTER 6:

LEADERSHIP BUY-IN MUST BE SEEN, NOT JUST HEARD

Here is a question we hear a lot: *Should change come from the bottom or the top of an organization?* People's answers differ, but the truth is that it doesn't matter. What matters is *how* change happens, not *where* it originates.

Ideally catalysts for innovation (and groundswells of opportunity) will ripple across your organization from every level and layer simultaneously. In other words, any organization that enjoys a decent degree of synergy likely will encounter the same opportunities across its various layers at roughly the same time. A CEO will thus become interested in a new technology or market opportunity just as other members of the organization stumble onto it (or were about to bring it to his or her attention).

This is ideal because, when this happens, no one has to fight to pitch the idea, defend it or waste time *selling* it. Everyone already is interested and wants to learn more, and the process becomes more about application, collaboration, education, and development, instead of pitching and selling. Skipping the process of pitching and selling a foreign concept to management allows the organization to move and react to it quicker and with clearer purpose.

As with *experience design*, this sort of discovery mechanism doesn't happen by accident. Innovative companies are innovative by design. Likewise, adaptive companies are adaptive by design. The companies that stand the best chance of remaining competitive over the next few decades are the ones that manage to *bake* innovation, adaptability and change management into their DNA, but that still isn't enough. We can't just leave it at the *what* of it. We also have to give you some insight into the *how*.

Let's have another look at our original question: *Should change come from the bottom or the top of an organization?* You probably now realize this was the wrong question all along. The right question is:

How does an organization bake innovation, adaptability and change into its DNA?

The answer is: *By deciding that is what it wants to do.*

SHOULD LEADERS WITHOUT A CLEAR VISION STEP ASIDE?

It doesn't matter if 50, 60 or even 90 percent of the organization wants something to happen. If the CEO isn't entirely sold on the importance of this critical business objective, if it isn't at the top of the company's list of priorities, it won't happen.

This type of objective, first and foremost, requires vision.

Second, for any vision to turn into reality, you need will. Without will, the vision will never grow into anything more than a pipe dream.

Third, every decision, investment, acquisition, partnership, and hire must help drive the company closer to making that vision a reality. The entire organization, from top to bottom, must be aligned to this objective and understand how everyone plays a part in realizing it.

If the CEO doesn't *own, drive*, and *build* this vision, forget it. Right from the start, the wrong CEO (or the right CEO with the wrong focus) will kill any company's hopes of baking innovation, adaptability and change into its DNA. Thus a CEO who is risk-averse, technology averse, has not interest in innovation, or who is technically challenged will not be able to accomplish this vision.

That isn't bad news, by the way. It's just a reality check. It is also a good way of separating *management* from *leadership*. CEOs who fall into the four above categories are not *change leaders*. They are, for our purposes, merely managers. That doesn't necessarily make them ineffective as CEOs, or in any way incompetent. It certainly doesn't make them bad people. There is nothing wrong with effectively *managing* a company... at least for a little while. It's just that the type of change, the type of *evolution* we are talking about in these chapters requires more than what they have to offer.

For any company to successfully manage a digital transformation and evolve into a player in the experience economy, traits like risk-aversion, technology-aversion and innovation-aversion are simply incompatible with the desired outcome.

CAN A TECH-CHALLENGED CEO DELEGATE CHANGE LEADERSHIP?

It is possible for a less than tech-savvy CEO to delegate the type of transformation we are talking about to a COO, CDO, a Chief Transformation Officer, or a capable team of change agents. But a delegating CEO must at least show a credible measure of clarity in regard to the company's vision, buy-in and passion. (The CEO doesn't have to physically drive, but the CEO does have to lead.)

Going back to our earlier discussion about Walt Disney, it is doubtful that, if Walt were alive today, he would understand exactly *how* RFID chips, wireless sensors, predictive modeling software, AI, and connected devices all work, but he would understand that they *do*. More importantly, he would understand that, used together, they have the power to deliver the magical experiences he always dreamed about. In regards to how these technologies might all be combined to solve problems, improve outcomes, and ultimately build dragons, he would most likely rely on his Chief Digital Officer, Chief Technical Officer, Chief Guest Experiences Officer and Chief Transformation Officer (among others), to make it happen.

Some of our conversations with digital executives in recent months have even touched on the notion that the digital leadership role might have to evolve from CDO (Chief Digital Officer) to CDTO (Chief Digital Transformation Officer). The evolving nature of digital being what it is, the operational shift from CDO to CDTO makes a lot of sense to us.

As a bonus, it also directly addresses the question of responsibility and ownership in the organization as it pertains to digital transformation. This can allow a CEO to safely take a delegating role in regards to digital transformation without appearing to be too hands off. This doesn't mean that the CEO should completely disconnect from the process. Delegation is ultimately about efficiency, nothing more.

To make sure that this kind of delegation doesn't go too far, here are some common traits and behaviors to look for in a delegating CEO. Even with an able CDTO managing the day to day of the company's digital transformation, the CEO should:

- Understand the need to create a dragon-building organization,
- Create a clear vision for the organization,
- Articulate that vision clearly and credibly,
- Drive the vision's execution by making the appropriate investments, hires and changes to the company,
- Speak with fluency and authority about the vision, the company's progress thus far, and its next steps,
- Demonstrate a fluency in the use and the articulation of value of the technologies and processes employed in the execution of said vision,
- Demonstrate a genuine passion and belief for the vision, and
- Be the vision's primary spokesperson and advocate.

BRIDGING THE GAP BETWEEN DELEGATING CEOS AND LEADER CEOS

Examples of clearly engaged CEOs whose companies are obviously focused on digital transformation, innovation and adaptability are:

- Apple's Steve Jobs,
- IBM's Ginni Rometty,
- Salesforce's Marc Benioff,
- Zappos's Tony Hsieh,
- Amazon's Jeff Bezos,
- SAP's Bill McDermott,
- Starbucks's Howard Schultz, and
- Space X's Elon Musk.

If you never have watched any of these CEOs speak to an audience about their companies and how they plan to pave the way for the next wave of innovation or growth, hop on over to YouTube, grab some popcorn and take the time to sit through any of their keynotes. What you will quickly note is the degree to which they understand *what* they are doing and *why*, the ease and fluency with which they can explain it, and the enthusiasm and belief that characterize the manner in which they articulate their dreams, ideas and insights.

What you learn by watching and listening to CEOs who are *fully* vested in baking innovation, adaptability and change into their companies' DNA is that they *believe* it is their most important duty as a CEO. They *know* the only real enemy of *any* business is complacency, and so they know their organizations' most critical strategic advantages over their competitors is the ability to evolve and transform better and faster. They *know* this. And, because they know it, they spend every day making sure that their organizations do whatever they have to do to stay as many steps ahead of their competitors as possible. They don't wait for someone to brief them on what might be lurking over the horizon; they make a point to go find out. They surround themselves with people who will find the answers to questions no one has thought to ask yet, and they task those people to build teams that can turn an idea or opportunity into something that will make the company better — a new product, service, channel, strategy, partnership, acquisition, tool, etc. They push past their own limitations, technical or otherwise, and find ways to build lean, focused, cutting edge, adaptable organizations.

The bottom line is this: *How* a CEO arrives at transforming a company isn't all that important. What matters is that they find a way to make it happen. As long as the will to innovate and evolve is there, the rest is just a matter of getting it done. That's good news because it means that leaders don't have to be particularly tech savvy to be successful. It helps if they are, obviously, and there always is room for improvement and growth, but CEOs *can* successfully lead their organizations' digital transformations without being technology experts. (You can breathe a sigh of relief now.)

CHAPTER 7:

BRINGING STRUCTURE TO DIGITAL TRANSFORMATION

Now that we reviewed some of the major pieces of the digital transformation puzzle, let's start putting them together. We will resist the temptation to try and provide you with a cookie-cutter action plan or roadmap because every company is different. There is no one-size-fits-all digital transformation model that will fit perfectly into everyone's world. What we want to do instead is bring together everything we have covered so far and give you some structure, clarity and guidance as to what should come next. First things first, some structure.

ENVISIONING YOUR DIGITAL TRANSFORMATION IN PHASES

The tricky thing about change-based processes like evolution, innovation and digital transformation is that they never really end. This is the one major difference between say planning to run your first marathon and using digital transformation to turn your company into an innovative, disruptive market leader. Sticking to our marathon analogy, the process we are outlining here doesn't end with the completion of that first marathon. It ends when your process of training for marathons allows you to run every marathon faster and better than the one before.

Let's break down this process into five phases:

PHASE 1: EXPERIENCE AS A PLATFORM

Shift from *product design* thinking to *experience design* thinking. Integrate experience design into your business model. Design new experiences into and around every touchpoint. Shift your opportunity matrix toward the potential of the experience economy. This is a transitional phase.

PHASE 2: DIGITAL ASSIMILATION

Bring digital thinking into every aspect of your business. This means that every digital and omnichannel practice that lives on the edges of your business needs to become part of your *core* business. This is the phase in which employee engagement and innovation becomes baked into your organization's DNA. This too is a transitional phase.

PHASE 3: SEAMLESS TECHNOLOGY ENABLEMENT

This is the phase in which new technologies become fully integrated into your business ecosystem. This means your investments in social, mobile, cloud solutions, SaaS, big data, AI, IoT, automation, and other key technologies are no longer piecemeal and haphazard. They are fully coordinated, seamless and easily upgradable. Your IT infrastructure is either hybridized (part legacy/in-house systems and part cloud-based systems) or entirely cloud-based. This technological transformation phase turns your company's technology infrastructure into an agile, adaptable and easily scalable *business enablement* platform. At this point technology is no longer a burden, it is a force-multiplier.

PHASE 4: OUTCOME ACCELERATION

Shift from educated guesses to data-driven insights and decisions. (This is where investments in cloud solutions, big data and AI start paying for themselves.) At this juncture, your company's continuous improvement model starts to feel effortless, technological integration because almost instinctive, and the discovery of new opportunities and your capacity for innovation start to feel natural. Change has become almost frictionless, which means that the speed at which you can analyze, decide, plan, and implement has reached its maximum velocity. This is no longer a transition phase. This is an *outcome acceleration* phase. Once you reach this phase in your digital transformation, your company's ability to *adapt, improve* and *innovate* finally outpaces that of your competitors. It is when you reach this phase that you finally begin to drive market disruption.

PHASE 5: DISRUPTION AS A MODEL

In this final phase of your transformation, your capacity for market disruption can be multiplied by a) partnering with key vendors, service providers, technology hubs, research labs, etc., *and* b) through key acquisitions, which generally focus on startups and other technology providers.

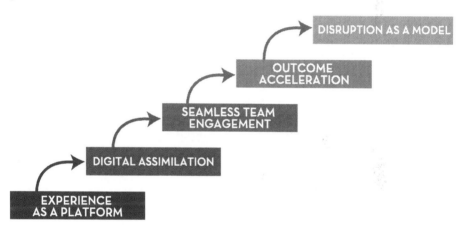

Fig. 7.1: **The 5 Phases of Digital Transformation**

Having a basic notion of what the five phases are should make creating a digital transformation roadmap for your company easier. Armed with this basic framework, you can plan each phase a little better, start developing your major milestones along the way and, of course, more easily communicate your vision to the rest of your organization.

Before we move on, there are some important additional considerations we need to cover. These are meant to help you identify key areas of focus and fill in the blanks, so to speak, as you begin to build your five-phase transformation plan.

ADDITIONAL INSIGHTS AND POINTS OF FOCUS:

1. **Drive customer to the core.** In the experience economy, customers interpret the value of your brand based on how they feel during and after every interaction (not just transactions) they have with it. With customers able to do their own research on companies and products now, and with the power to decide how they want to interact with brands, the balance of power has shifted in their favor. As digital has become the main vehicle for customers to connect with brands, brands must leverage it to engage customers. That is how they can balance the scales. Therefore, what used to be a "separate" digital strategy must become fully integrated into the core business and, in many ways, *drive* that core business. Physical and digital engagement with customers and markets must be consistent, seamless and as friction-free for customers as possible.

2. **Get executive-level buy-in.** Whether your company already has taken its first steps toward digital transformation or is beginning its journey, it will need executive buy-in to succeed. Once the *why*, *what* and *how* of the vision is established, focus on earning executive management approvals for technological innovation for the long-term. Sell the long play first. This may seem counterintuitive, since big change usually means big opposition, but you have to sell the entire journey (and the value of the destination) before you can start selling the milestones. Everyone at the top needs to understand where they are going and why they need to go there. Once they do, *then* start breaking the journey down into smaller goals, targets, projects, and milestones.

3. **Get companywide buy-in.** It isn't enough to sell leadership on the idea. You also have to sell the rest of the organization. Incentivizing initiative and participation in this endeavor is a good start. Setting goals and targets for milestones and achievements, personal and project-based, are good ways to build momentum. Recognizing and rewarding contributions, progress and success, close the loop (in a good way). Remember that to build an effective culture of transformation (or evolution, or change or innovation), you must also build a culture of celebration. The two go hand-in-hand. For the average employee, "change" means risk and uncertainty. To mitigate that, you need to flip that script. Turn change into an opportunity for growth, success, rewards, and celebration. If employees are tasked with building dragons, that becomes part of their job. Innovation isn't as risky to them personally anymore, and that frees them to innovate and push the limits of their own creativity.

4. **Identify and support your champions.** Every business, idea and project needs champions. These individuals usually are highly respected in an organization or industry and can help influence peers, employees and managers when it comes to any number of things, from pursuing innovative ideas to technological adoption. It is vital to identify these agents of change and empower them. It doesn't necessarily mean giving them carte blanche to do whatever they want (though that is certainly an option).

   Again, every company is different, so find the right balance, but the point is that the more champions you have, the more granular and widespread your leadership's connective tissue will be across the organization, and the smoother your digital transformation and dragon-building process will be. Incentivize these champions to reinforce the benefits of the changes (current or on the horizon), by allowing them to educate, guide and even inspire. The company with the most trusted advocates of change in place at all levels of the organization has a considerable advantage over companies that only have a few. More champions means less resistance to change, faster technological deployment across the company and a broader adoption of the notion that change is a net positive for everyone involved in it.

5. **Encourage innovation throughout the company.** The motivation to adopt new technology and the innovative ideas that take a business to the next level can come from any department in your organization. Instead of relying on focus groups, consultants or creatives to suggest the latest tech (or propose new ideas), open the floor to the entire company. Sometimes employees keep their heads down for fear of rocking the boat or sounding unsatisfied with the status quo. Creating a mechanism by which opportunities and ideas can flow freely will put an organization on a faster track to companywide innovation and it will accelerate digital transformation buy-in from employees. The trick is to *also* create a mechanism by which signal can be extracted from noise, or your organization will not be able to tell strong ideas from weak ones. (A healthy marketplace for ideas should naturally reward the best ideas and let the weaker ones fall by the wayside.)
   There are many ways of doing this, but the most successful we have seen involves *ideathons*. Ideathons should be deliberately small, short and frequent: 10-20 people maximum, rarely longer than 60-90 minutes and hosted every two to four weeks. They work like informal brainstorming sessions. (Never call them "meetings.") Employees are encouraged to present ideas to the group, either as individuals or small two- or three-person teams. They are given a short time (say

three minutes) to present their idea and sell the group on its purpose, value and feasibility. The group (composed of their peers and of one, two or three managers to keep things organized) votes on the ideas, and the group collectively selects the ones with the most potential (assuming any do). The top ideas are then selected to move on to the next round, during which the entire group collaborates to work out the kinks, propose fixes to whatever problems they encounter and help it move forward.

At the end of the process, theses ideas may be turned into actual project proposals that can be presented to management for consideration. (Or they can be sent back to the individual who proposed them and be worked on a little more, if they show promise but still need work.). These kinds of meetings are fast, fun, and cheap to host. A couple of boxes of donuts and some coffee are all you need to keep people's energy up during the process, and incentives/prizes can be put aside for submitting an idea, and/or having an idea selected for further analysis. (Just don't call this kind of program "ideas for donuts." It's catchy, sure, but it might send the wrong message.)

This model deployed across an organization can uncover more opportunities for business improvements and innovation than any focus group or consulting firm ever will. Let's call them "Bonuses."

Bonus 1: Group exercises like this boost morale and improve engagement.

Bonus 2: Group exercises like this also build team cohesion and teach employees to collaborate and regularly practice their critical problem solving skills together.

Bonus 3: These exercises train everyone who takes part to become natural co-innovators. As they mature in your organizations, these are the teams that will most likely help build more dragons in the future.

Bonus 4: These exercises are how you identify employees with promise. The donuts and prizes are nice, but don't stop there. Use these ideathons (you don't have to call them that) to spot talent that might not have been obvious to you before, give these insightful employees the opportunity to show you what they can do, and help them grow into the champions and future leaders they are likely to become. If their idea shows promise, help them flesh it out, present it to decision-makers and fight for it. Give them ownership in the project that will grow out of that idea. In other words, reward them not only with donuts but with real opportunity. Invest in them based on the opportunities they uncover themselves.

Before long, spontaneous collaborative innovation projects will start to sprout across the organization *without* the need for organized, scheduled ideathons (or whatever you call them). This is how you begin to build cultures of engagement and innovation in companies, and how opportunities to build more dragons will organically sprout across your organization.

6. **Test, test, test technology solutions, then prioritize ease of use.** Whenever companies bring new tools into their digital ecosystems, adoption can be a hurdle. To reduce internal friction and accelerate adoption of new technologies, plan small, strategic technology tests throughout your organization. For instance, try new software solutions. Demo and test-drive new CRM systems, business intelligence solutions, content management software, collaboration suites, and so on. Task every department with identifying new solutions and create a system by which they can easily partner with IT to test them out. If a solution seems like a good fit, expand the scope of the test. Before any kind of decision is made, or before a deployment, work with your managed service providers to set up test runs across your organization.

These tech tests serve four purposes. First, they build a culture of continuous improvement through trial-and-error into your organization, which reinforces that innovation and change are part of everyday life. Second, they empower employees. As they feel some degree of control over the selection of the tools they will use to best do their work (as opposed to having little say in the technologies they are forced to use), they will feel empowered to become partners in your journey of digital transformation. This is how you can begin to answer the "what's in it for us?" question. Empowered employees tend to be more engaged and comfortable with initiative and change than employees who feel they have little or no control over the management of their departments. Third, asking IT to *facilitate* these tests rather than *manage* them places less stress on IT's limited resources. Fourth, putting the testing of new solutions in the hands of the people most likely to use them significantly reduces the risk that a manager will select the wrong technology solution for his organization.

To maximize the potential for technological agility, minimize IT costs, and transition into a more mobile environment, lean toward a) cloud solutions (get familiar with cloud storage and application management) and b) embrace the value of remote work. (Independence from on-premise solutions is a good thing.) Mobile solutions also give IT departments more flexibility to troubleshoot, update, and monitor systems and solutions from anywhere. Making sure employees can easily update or install new apps and software on their devices (not just their work computers) makes their adoption and use much easier.

7. **Broaden your business objective horizons.** A company that focuses its digital transformation efforts mostly on customer acquisition is missing the point. Acquisition is only the first step. The *real* opportunity comes from repeat business (the longer the customer lifecycle, the better) and word-of-mouth (positive recommendations are gold). Acquisition is only the first of three parts. Next come customer development and customer retention — the stages during which you turn *like* into *love* and turn casual customers into *loyal* customers. This means that once the acquisition has taken place, every interaction with that new customer, every experience you create *for* and share *with* them should drive affection, trust, desire, and whatever other positive triggers are relevant to the journey you want them to embark on.

This process requires that you work to build (and nurture) a relationship with them every time they touch anything with your name on it, like a website, an app, a social feed, a product, the back of a box, the inside of a box, a checkout basket, their device's notification tray, a customer review, their email inbox, an in-store shopping experience, a customer service representative, or an ad. The goal is to keep delivering remarkable, magical experiences for them. Your digital transformation should focus on identifying, designing and creating a universe of unique, remarkable experiences that will become the hallmarks of your business and your brand.

These points should give you plenty to think about at this stage of your planning process.

CHAPTER 8:

WHY TRUST MUST PRECEDE TOOLS WHEN DRIVING DIGITAL TRANSFORMATION

Trust is a difficult topic to tackle in a book like this. For starters, it's a bit of an intangible. "Trust" means different things to different people. The meaning of "trust" changes from topic to topic. A consumer trusting a company with his or her personal data is a different conversation about trust than an employee trusting their CEO's ability to weather a crisis, for example. Having said that, we cannot ignore the importance that trust plays in a company's digital evolution (or any kind of evolution, really), as it acts as a bonding agent for the building blocks of that change or an impediment to it.

This may seem like a philosophical topic, but it really isn't. Trust is, at its core, about process — the process of building something that will work, understanding how all the pieces fit, and making sure you aren't leaving anything out. As our world (and economy) changes and evolves, trust can no longer be a bonus or an afterthought. Trust has to be built into our business models, relationships and identities. Trust, therefore, has to be understood through (and built into) the following entities:

• People,
• Roles,

- Technologies,
- Processes,
- Products,
- Services,
- Experiences, and
- Brands.

Building trust with people is easy to understand, so let's start with that one. As far back as we can go in human history, trust has been one of the most vital bonds between individuals. Trust is the one factor that makes you think of someone as an ally or an enemy, friend or foe, opportunity or threat. The more in common we have with someone, the more familiar we are with them, the more likely we are to trust them. We actually need to feel trust to form bonds. That need is hardwired into our brains. There is no getting around it. For an organization to be effective, everyone who is part of it has to trust the person to their right, the person to their left, and so on. An organization is, at its core, a social construct, much like a tribe. The more tribe-like an organization, in fact, the more engaged and productive it tends to be.

Trust is a prerequisite for human organization and collaboration. Let's apply our understanding of trust to *role identities* [29]. Everyone plays a role in someone else's life: mother, father, brother, sister, neighbor, friend, and so on. These roles come with certain expectations. We trust in the person, in the role they play in our lives, and in the implicit promise that they will meet our expectations of their duties or qualities in regard to their roles. We trust that *authority figures*, for instance, will not abuse their power by lying, betraying or taking advantage of us. When it comes to politics, we prefer *politicians* we think we can trust. In business and commerce, we prefer to do business with *salespeople* we trust. Our social and professional circles are built on trust. A coworker, manager, employee, or CEO is more than just a person. We are all incarnations of specific roles to different people and their trust in us (as our trust in them) is based upon whether we (or they) prove worthy of that trust.

We have moved from "Is this a trustworthy person?" to "Is this person a trustworthy industry analyst? Is this person a trustworthy manager? Is this person a trustworthy spokesperson? Is this person a trustworthy CEO?" If the answer is yes, carry on. If the answer is no, you probably need to do something about that.

Let's ask the same question we just asked of people and roles to

---

[29]Jackson, R. L., Hogg, M.A. (2010). *Encyclopedia of identity*. Thousand Oaks, CA: SAGE Publications.

technology. Is this technology trustworthy? Breaking it down a bit more, let's ask can we trust this technology to:

• actually solve the problem it promises to solve?
• be 100 percent reliable?
• not fail?
• not betray us in some way?
• be hacker and virus-proof?
• scale without business?

If trust in people (and in the roles they play) in an organization is so vital, and they are an essential building block of your organization, then the same must be true of technology. You have to be able to trust the technology you bring into your business the same way (and for the same reasons) that you trust your human assets. Cutting corners with technology yields the same types of problems as cutting corners with employee. The moment your organization starts losing trust in a technology solution is when it can be diagnosed with an operational cancer.

When we talk about digital transformation, the reflex often is to start with categories of technology and different types of tools, but this aspect of the transformation itself is often overlooked. Don't overlook it. If you get this part wrong, you will pay for it, and it won't be cheap or easy to fix. As with the old construction adage, *measure twice, cut once*, make sure that every piece of technology you bring into your world, whether it is employee-facing or customer-facing, is worthy of your trust. Although we have mentioned the importance of speed and "fast failing," it probably is better to slow the pace of your digital transformation and get it right the first time than it is to mess this up and teach your employees and customers to wonder if every change you make to their world is something they can securely embrace or look upon with suspicion and worry.

The same is true of your processes. When processes work, employees learn to accept and trust them. Remember that trust accelerates adoption. That's because trust pushes aside barriers and friction, because it minimizes doubt and caution. If you focus on building consistently effective processes and methodologies inside your organization, employees will learn to trust your ability to do so and accept change faster and with less resistance. We will talk a little more about change management in the next chapter, so we aren't done with this topic. Just know that when it comes to change management, which helps drive *adaptation* and digital transformation, trust can either be your worst enemy or your ally. Less trust equals friction, hurdles and obstacles to change. More trust means smooth, fast and painless change.

When it comes to products, services, experiences, and brands, the same thing applies. Nobody wants to buy a product or service they can't trust, especially from a company they don't think they can't trust. It's also difficult to imagine anyone wanting to commit to an *experience* they can't trust. (Nobody likes to be lied to or betrayed, so imagine expecting people to pay for the privilege.) *Trust* then has to be baked into every aspect of a business, not just internally so the wheels and gears will go round and round like they are supposed to, but externally as well. In fact, trust in many ways is part of a subconscious experience design. Brands, whether they operate in B2C, B2B, B2G or G2E (Government to everything), have to make sure trust is baked into every fiber of their business. Trust is the single most important asset a brand has at its disposal. It is at the heart of its *reputation*, and as brands take on roles in our lives, public trust is predicated entirely on a brand's ability to meet the expectations of its market. Reward that trust and you are golden. Betray it, or fall short of it, and it doesn't matter what else you do.

The flip side of *trust* as a significant market differentiator is its fragility. Trust is as difficult to build than it is to break, and, once broken, it is remarkably difficult to repair. This imbalance makes it all the more important that leaders (and the organizations they build and manage) treat it with the utmost care, respect and attention. That is why it cannot be an afterthought, and why we decided it was important to dedicate a chapter to it in this book.

As you move forward through the phases of your digital transformation, remember to consider the impact that every decision you make will have on trust. Decisions to consider in relation to trust include:

- A new hire,
- Social engagement,
- An advertisement,
- A new product or service,
- A new payment system or checkout solution,
- A new technology solution,
- Deeper access to customer data,
- A press release,
- Corporate transparency guidelines, and
- A promise made to employees, investors or customers.

Will your choices risk costing you that hard-earned trust or will they contribute to building more of it? Every choice falls into one or the other category, so make sure not to leave that particular aspect of your transformation to chance.

Ultimately, the model you want to build is simple:

1. Trust in who you are as a leader, in your purpose, in your vision, in the process, in improvement, and in your ability to make informed and timely course corrections along the way. Hire well. Celebrate every success. Reward the right things. Learn to treat failures as opportunities to improve.

2. Build an *internal* culture of trust. Trust in a common, shared purpose. Trust in the leadership team's ability to navigate uncertain waters skillfully and successfully. Trust in the entire tribe's drive, dedication and competence. Trust in the *right* technologies and processes. Trust in the genius of your products and services. Trust in every aspect of your business because you built it right and continue to do so.

3. Build an *external* culture of trust. Trust in the brand's purpose, cause or mission. Trust in its direction, the company's leadership, and the company's advertising and marketing. Trust in the company's salespeople and other customer-facing touchpoints. Increasingly, that trust must also focus on the company's ability to keep customer data from falling into the wrong hands. That means top-of-the-line firewalls and security software, advanced encryption and whatever it takes to earn the trust of the general public in ways that were not on consumers' or analysts' radars 10 years ago.

If, moving forward, you don't know what kind of culture you should build besides a culture of innovation, just build a culture of trust. It doesn't matter what industry you're in or how big or small your business is, you can't go wrong with that.

CHAPTER 9:

BUILDING CULTURES OF CELEBRATION

A critical aspect of planning (and facilitating) any long and complex journey is to break that journey down into manageable portions. It doesn't matter if you are training for a triathlon, planning a cross country road trip with the family, driving an organization's digital transformation, or turning your company into a dragon.

Quick progress check: By this point, you should have a few objectives and opportunities in mind and be able to roughly articulate where your company should be in three to five years compared to where it is today.

If you are reading this book for the first time and haven't yet made a list of the technologies and competencies you will need to invest in (or a timeline of their adoption and deployment), that's all right. We will get to that. This chapter will outline some basic principles you can build on later anyway, so just absorb what you can now, take a few notes and come back to it later. If this is *not* your first time reading this book, you should have a fairly layered, fleshed out vision for what the next three to five years will look like (and maybe even the next ten). Being able to draw from that degree of specificity will be helpful at this juncture. Wherever you may be in your journey or planning, read on.

Once you have outlined your vision for where you want the company to be in three to five years, start small. Focus on incremental improvements, things you can fix, improve or build quickly, cheaply and with minimal risk of failure.

You always want to keep your first round of wins deliberately small and achievable. This will warm your organization up a little before tackling big, complex and potentially risky projects. For now, let your project teams learn how to work together. Respect their natural learning curves. Let them settle into their own rhythm and work out the wrinkles. At first, think of it as the smaller and the more manageable the project, the better.

EMPOWERING EMPLOYEES: THE DIFFERENCE BETWEEN CULTURES OF REWARDS AND CULTURES OF CELEBRATION

Every time one of your teams succeeds, recognize its achievement, put it in context for the rest of the organization (explain how it fits into your digital transformation), and reward it in a *meaningful* way. (Warning: A $25 gift card to everyone's favorite coffee chain may not qualify as *meaningful*.) It is important to do all three because there is a difference between building *cultures of rewards* and *cultures of celebration*.

Cultures of rewards are driven by incentives: bonuses, commissions, contests, and so on. Cultures of celebration, however, while focused on rewarding for performance, *also* incorporate the value of working toward a *shared mission* to their success equation. In these cultures, contributing to the organization's improvement, evolution and transformation, *being part* of something bigger is treated as a reward in and of itself. (It is an incentive *and* a driver of engagement.) The psychology behind it is simple — everyone wants to feel valued. Everyone wants to be acknowledged for their role and place in an organization that they can feel they own a piece of, even when that piece is a tiny part in its success.

Never underestimate the power of pride in a job well done, in the feeling of achievement that comes with having helped one's team succeed and in the powerful need most people have to *belong* to a group. That is why building projects and companies around a *shared mission* is so powerful (as opposed to "maximizing shareholder value," for instance, or chasing a 3 percent raise).

Shared mission and what the military might call *unit cohesion.* These are the sorts of things that drive employees to be engaged and productive. Take that away from them, or forget to empower them at all, and you will teach them to work for themselves and focus on their own individual goals. Organizations that don't get this part of the culture equation right typically struggle to drive productivity, initiative and collaboration, and, without them, transformation and change are nearly impossible.

To make any kind of digital transformation possible, you *must* learn to connect individual employees and teams to your shared purpose and make that shared purpose theirs. Give them ownership in it, and, when the time comes, help them celebrate their achievements and wins.

How is this done? Their contributions and achievements must have a clear value to the organization (and in our case, to our journey of digital transformation). This means their contributions have to be acknowledged, shared and celebrated.

RANDOMNESS VS. BUILDING BLOCKS, MILESTONES, AND THE IMPORTANCE OF CELEBRATING THE RIGHT THINGS

We are not talking about handing out gold stars to everyone just for doing their jobs. An organization that celebrates everything celebrates nothing. But, as we move toward building a new version of your company, a *better* version of your company, every step of that building process matters, and every proverbial brick you lay to that end deserves its own acknowledgment, celebration and reward. So how do you make sense of it all? How do you know what to celebrate?

The simplest way to do this is to break down every step of the process into specific building blocks and milestones, and plot these on a roadmap that everyone can see and understand. Thus, A leads to B leads to C leads to D, and so on. As the company moves from building block to building block and from milestone to milestone, every notable, metered achievement along that roadmap of progress is cause for celebration, and the persons who worked to move things to this point are recognized. No building block or milestone is too small or insignificant in a culture of celebration. The success of this model hinges on an organization's ability to identify clear, achievable milestones, drive progress from one to the next and celebrate progress accordingly.

We mention this not because it is a "new" or revolutionary concept (it is neither), but because most organizations either forget to take advantage of it or don't take the time to. As a result, their journeys of digital transformation tend to be filled with false starts, friction, resistance, and failure. When you look at companies that make a point of incorporating these insights into their operational models, however (their "culture") you notice that progress comes much more smoothly. (Look for any list detailing "the best companies to work for" and you will notice that most, if not all of them, also happen to be innovative, dynamic and ahead of their competitors in all things tech. This is not a coincidence.)

Building the right culture is as vital to your success in turning your company into a dragon as building the right IT infrastructure is to driving an organization's digital transformation.

MILESTONES, GOALS AND CRITERIA FOR CELEBRATION

Criteria for celebration can vary from company to company, so here is a short list of questions to guide you as you work to identify types of contributions or achievement that warrant acknowledgment and/or celebration:

- Does this achievement constitute an improvement for the company?
- Does this achievement contribute to our journey of digital transformation?
- Is this achievement a minor milestone or a major milestone in that journey?
- How much resistance did those involved have to overcome to get this done?
- Were goals merely met or exceeded?

One quick word about goals: Always be specific when setting goals. Set parameters. Define them as specific targets with specific metrics. Every goal should have a spec sheet or a list of criteria and deliverables to be met. If, upon delivery, nine out of 10 of those deliverables have not been met, the milestone as a whole was not met. Don't cut corners. Don't sell yourself short. In this particular journey, it is more important to get the content of the milestones right than to meet a deadline. No one will really notice if you improve your omnichannel experience two weeks behind schedule, but they will notice if your improvement is glitchy or only works 80 percent of the time. Celebrations and achievements are only meaningful when they don't cut corners.

MAKING SURE GOALS COEXIST, BUT DON'T INTERFERE WITH ONE ANOTHER

If digital transformation truly is a priority for your company, don't treat is as a primary goal or objective at the beginning of a quarter and as a secondary goal or objective toward the end of that quarter when competing business objectives suddenly need to be met.

One of the worst traps organizations fall into when adding a digital transformation journey into their model is creating competition between business goals. Meeting a digital transformation milestone cannot compete with a quarterly sales goal, for instance. This doesn't mean that they cannot *coexist* as goals (they probably should), but that they cannot *compete* against one another. Never put a manager in a position to have to *choose* between meeting a quarterly sales goal and reaching a digital transformation milestone. That is a sign of poor planning and poor resource allocation, and it sends mixed signals to your organization in regard to how serious you are about your journey of transformation.

With adequate planning and commitment, this doesn't have to be a problem, but be sure to do what is necessary not to fall into this trap.

FINAL THOUGHTS

Here are a few final thoughts about celebrations that we want to leave you with:

1. Big milestones should result in big celebrations. Small milestones lead to smaller celebrations. All milestones and celebrations should be meaningful, but proportionality *is* a language. For your culture of celebration to be credible and effective, celebrations should match the importance of what it is you are celebrating. Context is important.

2. Celebrate teams *and* individuals. This isn't necessarily an exercise in voting for an MVP (which can actually be counterproductive). Instead, consider asking every team leader to identify specific contributions made by each member of the team and recognizing that particular contribution as the milestone or achievement is celebrated. Perhaps

Jane worked 18 hours straight to get a website back up, or Ken had a brilliant idea that got the team unstuck, or Pradip put twice as many hours into the project as anyone else on the team... whatever that special contribution is, acknowledge and celebrate it. Do not underestimate the importance of tying individuals to team wins.

3. Starting the day with celebrations and good news carries a lot more weight than waiting until later in the day or celebrating away from the office. Make the most out of your culture of celebration. Start the day with wins and accolades. (You can always celebrate again later.)

Getting your organization to a point where it can build dragons takes a little bit of front-end work, but nothing will get you there faster than combining a building-block type of process with a culture of celebration. State your objective, make it a common goal, create a simple roadmap, reward your people for the right behaviors and achievements, and do what you can to help them get there as fast and painlessly as possible. Do these things, and your team will amaze you.

CHAPTER 10:

SOCIAL BUSINESS FROM THE INSIDE OUT

It is nearly impossible to talk about digital transformation without talking about social media, or rather *social business*. What is the difference? For starters, when we talk about *social media*, we are talking about channels and platforms — Facebook, Twitter, YouTube, Instagram, Snapchat, and so on. *Social business*, however, refers to:

1. Any business function (or business model) specifically adapted to leverage social technologies to meet its objectives, and/or
2. Any business management philosophy that leverages social technologies to *humanize* itself and engage with an audience.

Ideally a social business manages to simultaneously become more human, authentic and transparent *and* take advantage of social platforms to improve every aspect of its operations, from customer service to sales. In the early days of social media, pioneers in this aspect of digital transformation leveraged social channels to accomplish the following:

• Build an audience,
• Build trust,

- Increase mindshare,
- Educate and entertain,
- Improve brand or product discovery (lead generation),
- Acquire new customers,
- Drive positive word of mouth and peer-to-peer recommendations,
- Drive repeat transactions from existing customers,
- Increase sales revenue,
- Increase marketing ROI,
- Recognize and empower super fans,
- Identify common pain points for customers,
- Improve the reach of their marketing and advertising, and
- Improve customer service.

Every objective on the list is a *business* objective, with or without social media. Nowhere on the list do we bring up *likes, shares* and *comments* as objectives or measures of success. That is because social business, as social and humanized as it may be, remains focused on *business*. Conversations with fans and customers can be friendly and genuine, they can be about kitten videos and whose team won the night before, but, ultimately, the underpinning of every relationship between a brand on social channels and its primary audience is a *business* relationship. This doesn't make a brand's social media accounts hypocritical or underhanded, by the way. Friendly service and building relationships with customers (offline or online) always has been part of doing business. All social channels do is add a *digital* dimension to what already was happening in retail stores, on the phone and by mail.

WHY SOCIAL BUSINESS IS IMPORTANT TO DIGITAL TRANSFORMATION

Think of social media platforms, channels, networks, and communities as a massive digital ecosystem that connects people to:

- Each other,
- Knowledge and ideas,
- Tribes and communities,
- Companies and brands,
- Products and services,
- News,
- Entertainment,
- Technology, and
- Experiences.

This ecosystem is a vast and layered digital marketplace. Once you see "social media" as a marketplace rather than just "channels," its importance becomes a lot clearer. Bonus: Understanding that social media is a marketplace gives you some indication of what, as a business, you should do there.

When you see a company working to build a *social business*, you know someone there understands that the social space is a marketplace and it brings massive business opportunities with it. (Facebook alone is moving toward the 2 billion active user mark, and it is only one of many players.) Integrating *social* into your business is a vital component of any digital transformation.

Understanding that social is a market and *doing* something about it are two different things. When it comes from moving from understanding to doing, in spite of what you may have heard from legions of social media "experts," building a social business isn't as simple as opening up accounts on various social networks, randomly "engaging" with "fans," and pushing out marketing content every 2.7 hours. It is also *not* something you can or should hand off to an intern. (We would not have to make a point to mention this if so many companies, large and small, were not still doing exactly that.)

For any social business to be successful, it requires a vision, a plan and capable resources. Building a social business practice is not an afterthought or an add-on. It has to be taken seriously to be successful.

To stay out of trouble, let's set a few ground rules regarding every element of your digital transformation (especially the ones you should prioritize):

1. Always have a point,
2. Always have a plan and
3. Never cut corners.

Let's go back to basics for a minute, just to be sure we didn't miss anything along the way:

Question: What is the point of building a social business (and by "point," we mean *purpose*)?
Answer: The point is to become a better company. (See Chapters 1-3.)

Question: How do we become a better company?
Answer: By eliminating pain points and delivering the best experiences we can.

Question: How does building a social business help us accomplish any of that?

Answer: Start with the list of business objectives at the beginning of this chapter and add your own.

Let's focus on two opportunities in particular though, because they are promising for most companies.

Seeing, hearing and knowing everything. First, social channels are essentially giant windows into customer and market insights. All day long, hundreds of millions of people share their likes and dislike, take pictures of what food they eat, what cars they wish they could drive, what gadgets they wish they could buy, what parts of the world they dream of visiting, and so on. Everything you have ever wanted to know about a market is right there for you to capture, analyze and turn into insights (and opportunities). We'll come back to that in Chapter 12 when we discuss how cloud technologies and artificial intelligence can help companies crunch big data and turn it into actionable insights. All you need to remember for now is that social media as an ecosystem is a massive real-time source of relevant and actionable insight into what to fix, what to build, what to sell, and to whom and when (among other things). The most important aspect of building a social business, then, is building a listening practice that captures information and data across social media channels.

Creating seamless, human, friendly interactions with customers. Second, before focusing on pushing out content and using social channels as marketing channels, invest in the unique humanization opportunity they offer. It isn't to say that you can't or shouldn't use social channels to advertise and market to people, but that isn't what you should focus on in your social feeds. Your focus, in the interest of creating remarkable experiences for your customers and prospects, should be to... well, create remarkable experiences for your customers and prospects. The easiest and cheapest way to do that is to focus on creating seamless, human, friendly interactions with customers. Here are a few examples:

1. **Customer Support:** Dedicate a customer service or customer support resource to key social channels. Any complaint or question regarding your company or one of your products can be captured automatically, turned into a customer service ticket and addressed by that resource. Depending on the size of your business and the number of complaints and questions you receive per hour, this function can be handled by one employee or several dozen.

2. **Community Management:** Sometimes just having someone online to help customers navigate your company's website, get the most out of your products or just help keep your brand front of mind is all you need to keep fans engaged. An engaging community manager, by virtue of being the human connector between an audience of prospects and your brand, can help prospects make their first purchase, for instance, or choose your brand over another. They can help fill the empty spaces between great web/mobile design and seamless checkouts. They also can help customers feel good about their purchases by validating their choices and helping them celebrate their purchases. (This is part of the culture of celebration we were just talking about in Chapter 9.)

Community management injects human relationships into an otherwise human-free digital or mobile experience. That social, human, relationship-centric element is *vital* if your brand wants to develop relationships with customers and nurture loyalty over time. Remember, we are focused on *experiences*, not just *design*. Even if your digital experience is beautiful and flawless, adding a little human touch can go a long way toward fulfilling an instinctive need for human connection, loyalty and trust.

3. **Special Services:** These are services that tend to be industry-specific. For example, if you are building a social business practice for a hotel chain, consider using social channels to connect customers to a virtual concierge, a housekeeping service or someone who can help them get around a city they aren't familiar with. If you are an airline, consider using social channels to quickly help travelers with common problem, like retrieving a lost item, inquiring about the departure status of a connecting flight or determining which restaurants in Terminal A cater to vegetarians. If you own a chain of retail stores, consider using social channels to help shoppers find gifts for loved ones, pair accessories to outfits, or provide them with fact sheets that will help them decide between Product A and Product B.

You are only limited by your own ingenuity and willingness to be helpful. It doesn't matter if you are a boutique retailer, an amusement park, an engineering firm, a news outlet, or a sports management agency — social channels can be leveraged to help you create seamless, human, friendly interactions with customers, and that is exactly how you should use them.

WHAT ABOUT SALES?

In the early days of social media, social selling was incongruous and difficult to execute smoothly. That is no longer the case today. Virtually every social platform today allows businesses to create ads (or post social content) that allows a potential customer to access a sales page or trigger a transaction with a single click. As long as a hyperlink can be embedded in an image, a piece of copy, or a pixel, any piece of content can be a link to a sales page. It doesn't matter much if you are selling cars, electronics, books, or services.

Just remember to balance social engagement and social selling. On micro blogging platforms like Twitter, for instance, some companies create separate accounts for different uses. Some are engagement-focused accounts (interactions between people) and some are transaction-driven accounts. Dell picked up on this opportunity early. Most of Dell's Twitter accounts are focused on engagement and education, but its @ DellOutlet account focuses exclusively on connecting Twitter followers to refurbished Dell products. By separating the feeds, Dell effectively manages to keep social selling and engagement separate. Smart move.

Keeping social engagement and social selling separate on other channels (like Facebook, YouTube and Instagram, for example) is less important than it is on Twitter. That is because the more layered a page's layout, the more it can separate genuine content from ads and other offers.

Bottom-line: Every channel and platform is different, but, as you familiarize yourself with each one, finding the ideal balance between engagement and social selling just becomes a matter of testing, measuring and optimizing, all of which can be done on the fly.

Just remember that, with the exception of paid ads, social selling is dependent on the size of your audience on any particular social channel and that audience's willingness to be marketed to. This means, for social selling to be effective, you have to first build an audience and make sure they won't be turned off when you inject your conversations with the occasional sales pitches. Again, context matters here. A poorly worded or timed sales pitch can raise some eyebrows. That is why so much of this chapter is dedicated to approaching social business with the right focus and plan.

Quick social selling rules to remember:

1. Relationship value is NOT transactional value.
2. Use social channels to *differentiate* yourself from your competitors, not just to sell alongside them.
3. Social credibility and social trust are more important than social selling.
4. Lead with building real value and positive experiences for your audience through engagement, helpful interactions, education, and entertainment.
5. Whenever possible, keep social selling to ads and/or dedicated social accounts, as to not interfere with your audience's expectations and trust.
6. Work to transition from *audience* to *community*.

A FINAL CONSIDERATION: BARRIERS OF ENTRY

As social technologies have reached a certain degree of maturity, they have become remarkably simple to use. There are virtually no barriers of entry for businesses. Social accounts are easy to create and manage. Digital professionals can easily customize their look and feel. For convenience, performance metrics and data are increasingly built into social platforms, and these reports are relatively easy to export. Even advertising on social channels (to grow followers or drive traffic directly to a company page) has become so simple that any digital professional can create an ad campaign in less than 20 minutes. There are virtually zero technical barriers of entry when it comes to building a social business.

Social platforms already come with their own publishing, advertising, search, and measurement functions, and that's fine, but they can also be connected to advanced software products that turn them into "Super platforms." Data from social channels, for example, can be organized and pushed in real time to elaborate dashboards, interactive data visualizations, word clouds, heat maps, and so on. You can, at the swipe of a fingertip, see every mention of your company around the world, by channel, in the last five minutes. You can, at the swipe of a fingertip, separate these mentions by positive or negative sentiment. You can replace that map with mentions that suggest purchase intent. In seconds, and with minimal training, you can, if you so wish, generate a report showing every Twitter account in the New York metropolitan area in the last two weeks that appears to be considering purchasing your product. We are getting a little ahead of ourselves here (we have once again crossed into the interwoven world of big data, cloud computing and artificial intelligence), but the point we are trying to make is this — as complicated and out of reach as this all sounds, it is neither. The types of digital tools already available today — tools that can transform a business into a social business, and a social business into a leading digitally transformed business — are surprisingly simple to use. The barriers of entry are limited to a short list:

1. Cost (some of these advanced tools are designed for the enterprise, so they can be a little pricy for small businesses),
2. Your IT department's technical competency,
3. The adaptability of your existing technology infrastructure,
4. Where you happen to be in your digital transformation, and
5. Regulatory hurdles. (Certain industries may have limitations as to how you may and may not use social technologies.)

That's it though. You only need to worry about five types of barriers of entry, and none is particularly difficult to adapt to, let alone insurmountable. They fall more into the speed bump category than actual hurdles. Here's how you solve these issues:

- If some tools are out of your price range, either raise capital or go with more cost-effective versions (or equivalents) of those tools. Just about everything else in the social marketplace is actually pretty inexpensive.
- If your IT department isn't capable of helping you get the most use out of social technologies, hire staff whose competencies align with the future, not the past.
- If your existing technology infrastructure cannot adapt to change, change your technology infrastructure. (We are going to talk about mobile and cloud later, so hold that thought.)
- If your digital transformation hasn't quite caught up to what your next key area of focus is, commit more resources to the project and move toward it faster.
- Regulatory hurdles aren't really hurdles. They're just rules. Learn them, build your practice around them and carry on.

Any business can, with a vision, the right plan and through the application of discipline, build a digital version of itself that will effectively leverage the social space.

Coffee shops, airlines, auto repair shops, taxi cab companies, universities, fashion brands, tech startups, municipal governments... you name it, they all do it, and, if many do it exceedingly well, so can you. It doesn't matter what your industry is, whether your market is B2B, B2C, B2G or something else, or if you are a one-person operation or a global brand with tens of thousands of employees throughout the world, the social space is a digital marketplace, and you need to be *in* it. Your best bet if you want to tap its full potential is to take that marketplace *as* seriously as you have every other marketplace you already focus on.

Whatever you do, don't let thousands of social media "experts," gurus and bloggers fool you into thinking that social media is not a legitimate marketplace or that *likes* and *shares* or *social influence* magically equate to ROI. Don't let any previous false starts discourage you from trying again (the right way this time). And whatever you do, don't let vacuous case studies distract you from the real opportunities that abound in this dynamic marketplace. If you miss or discount this piece of the digital equation, everything else you try to do will be more difficult than necessary. Have a point, have a plan and don't cut any corners.

CHAPTER 11:

IT ISN'T ABOUT MOBILE. IT'S ABOUT MOBILITY

When we originally drew the outline for this chapter, we thought about running through a history of mobility, wireless phones and pocket computers... but there is really no need for any of that. This chapter isn't really about "mobile." It's about mobility, which is different.

Forget for a moment that we are talking about mobile phones. In fact, forget that we are taking about phones at all. What we really are talking about, at least for now, is devices we carry with us everywhere, that wirelessly tether us to the rest of the world. It doesn't matter much whether those devices are hand-held little rectangles of plastic and glass, oblong little oysters that fold open and shut, wrist computers that look like watches, or eyeglasses with extra bits and pieces. What matters is this: Wherever we go, however far from home or the office we may be, those devices allow us to stay connected to each other, to our jobs, to news alerts, to information, to entertainment, and whatever else has value to us. This, by the way, obviously includes digital marketplaces like the social space, online shopping, and email.

It is tempting to spend some time talking about the growth of mobile in the world and show you stats and figures, but, since you can search for those stats and charts on your own (yes, on your mobile device), it makes more sense for us to distill this all to a few crucial and more useful points.

The world is divided into two major groups of mobile device users. The first group comprises users of mobile devices with an Internet connection (mobile web users). The second group comprises users of mobile phones with no connection to the Internet. (Most tend to live in economies and areas were broadband services are still lagging, but even that is a temporary hurdle.) To give you a sense of the global scale of mobile adoption and the size difference between these two groups, here are some quick figures that hopefully won't become obsolete too quickly:

- According to Cisco's 2015-2020 Virtual Networking Index and Global Mobile Data Traffic Forecast, 70 percent of the global population (or 5.5 billion people) will use a mobile device by 2020. [30]

- Of those, 72 percent will belong to the first group (mobile devices connected to the web), and the remaining 28 percent will belong to the second group (mobile devices with no Internet connection). [31]

If this doesn't seem that impressive, consider that in 2015, when we first started discussing this book, only 36 percent of the world's mobile users belonged to the first group. If the speed with which mobile adoption is occurring around the world doesn't sound an opportunity, the impact this will have on global marketplaces and consumer behaviors should. The surge of mobile adoption around the world is driving an eightfold increase in data usage between 2015 and 2020 [32]. Mobile has become so important to consumers that by 2020 (let's go ahead and keep the date consistent so we're all on the same timeline), more people will have mobile devices than electricity, running water and cars. Only 3.5 billion people will have running water, but 5.5 billion people will have a mobile phone in 2020 [33]. That's how important mobile devices are to people (and how much more economically accessible they are than we might have expected only a decade ago). Mobile is a massive driver of digital change across the world and it is basically a game-changer for civilization, just like the Internet.

This is not a discussion about iPhone vs. Droid, or specific device features, or apps, or screen sensitivity, but a discussion about mobility, which is another term for *connection*. The purpose of this chapter is

[30]*Cisco Visual Networking Index 2015-2020* [PDF]. (2016, February). Cisco.
[31]*Cisco Visual Networking Index 2015-2020* [PDF]. (2016, February). Cisco.
[32]Cisco. (2016, February 3). Cisco Visual Networking Index: Global Mobile Data Traffic Forecast Update, 2015–2020 White Paper. http://www.cisco.com/c/en/us/solutions/collateral/service-provider/visual-networking-index-vni/mobile-white-paper-c11-520862.html
[33]Cheng, R., CNET (2016, February 3). By 2020, more people will own a phone than have electricity. http://www.cnet.com/news/by-2020-more-people-will-own-a-phone-than-have-electricity/

to give you a better perspective when it comes to 1) how connected the world is becoming, and 2) how quickly marketplaces are adapting to mobile devices and the reality of always-connected consumers, and how quickly they are shifting the landscape of their expectations, especially in regards to experiences.

ESTABLISHING A BASELINE FOR ADAPTATION

Before we go any further, here are two questions you need to seriously consider (and try to answer):

- Is your company on the leading edge of mobile commerce?
- Is your company on the leading edge of mobile experiences?

If the answer to both is *yes*, congratulations! You probably don't need to read this chapter at all and may skip ahead. If the answer to either (or both) is *no*, then you have two more objectives to add to your digital transformation:

- How do we become our industry's leader in mobile commerce?
- How do we become our industry's leader in mobile experiences?

That journey, like many others, starts the moment someone raises their hand and asks the right question.

Desktop and laptop computers aren't dead or dying, at least not anytime soon, but other devices are taking over as the interface of choice for consumers. You don't need data and statistics to see the change. All you have to do is look around. Everyone is holding a phone in their hand and swiping at it. It doesn't matter if they are at their desks, on the bus, walking down the street, on the subway, in their cars, on the couch, at the restaurant, in the bathroom, on the plane, or sitting by a campfire. Everyone is checking their emails, scrolling through their Facebook newsfeed, checking Snapchat, posting selfies, streaming videos, searching for products, keeping up with friends, reading the latest news, paying their bills, planning their next vacation, and buying stuff.

Today's mobile device is a wallet, computer, TV, radio, newspaper, library, camera, gaming platform, classroom, shopping mall, remote control for your entire house, surveillance system for your pets, personal assistant, and so on. And, it becomes more every day. As John Boiler, founder of 72andSunny put it: "Smartphones have even become surrogate sales assistants. [34]" However indispensible mobile devices are as you read this book, imagine how much more indispensible and powerful they will be in five, 10 and 20 years.

The screen in their hand, on their wrist or projected onto their eyeball is the screen through which 5.5 billion people, in just a few years, will interface with every market you play in. It will be the access point via which more than 90 percent of every digital interaction between consumers (and probably your employees) and your company will take place. [35]

Think about that.

BREAKING DOWN THE MOBILE ELEMENT OF YOUR DIGITAL TRANSFORMATION

So the question is this: Are you ready? Are you already taking the necessary steps to adapt to this change? Has your company's journey of digital transformation taken this massive technological groundswell into account? Because we aren't talking about something that is 10 or 20 years down the road anymore. It's happening now. If you aren't already racing to get in front of this, your inability to adapt to it quickly enough will be devastating.

Remember what we said about weathering change at the beginning of this book. Reaction to change comes in two modes: 1) *Adapt or die*, which is defensive, and 2) *Disrupt or lose*, which is more offensive and initiative-driven.

At this juncture, it may be useful to organize your mobile strategy in three ways:

1. Establish a timeline for adaptation.

For now, think of your mobile strategy as a three-to-five year timeline. Visualize it (or better yet, draw it) and think about where you are now. Think about where you aren't. Think about all of the things your competitors are doing that you aren't. Think about what your competitors aren't doing but should be. Think about opportunity. Take your time. No idea is a bad idea at this point. What could you do better? What could you do to leverage mobile technologies to create better experiences for your customers? How could you use mobile

---

[34]Boiler, J. (2015, February). The Convergence of Retail and Mobile. https://www.thinkwithgoogle.com/shortlists/convergence-of-retail-and-mobile.html
[35]Cisco. (2016, February 3). Cisco Visual Networking Index: Global Mobile Data Traffic Forecast Update, 2015–2020 White Paper. http://www.cisco.com/c/en/us/solutions/collateral/service-provider/visual-networking-index-vni/mobile-white-paper-c11-520862.html

technologies to acquire, develop and retain customers? How could you use mobile technologies to accelerate product adoption, increase buy rates, and so on? Make a list.

Now think about what you want your company's mobile strategy to look like in six months, 18 months, 24 months, 30 months, 36 months, 40 months, 48 months, and 60 months. Note that the intervals we just suggested are not regular. That isn't an accident. Sticking to six- and 12-month intervals is too rigid, too boxed-in. Allow your innovation (and deployment) process to breathe a little. Let it settle into short and long cycles. This may interfere a bit with quarterly reports, but that is a good thing. Decisions made based on quarterly reports and schedules tend to be the wrong decisions for the wrong reasons. (Remember rule No. 3: Don't cut corners. The trick to doing that is to not put yourself in a position where you must make an arbitrary deadline that has nothing to do with a project's natural timeline.) Plot those points on your timeline and start your mobile evolution. It will take a lot of trial and error to finally get it right, but that's the point. This piece of the puzzle can be fun, but it is difficult. Just think about how much more difficult (and doomed to fail) it would be if you tried to wing it without going through this process.

2. Divide mobile between *adaptive* and *innovative* initiatives.

Divide all of your mobile initiatives into two categories. The first category will include adaptive, "catching-up" measures. The second category will include innovative "surging forward" initiatives that will give you an edge over your competition. A lot of initiatives that will fall into the second category probably won't even occur to you until you have reached Phase 3 of your digital transformation, so focus on the first category and catching up first. As you begin to catch up though, and make mobile an integral part of your business, ideas for more innovative and proactive mobile initiatives will start to bubble up for you.

One of the benefits of splitting your mobile initiatives between "catching up" and "surging forward" categories is that, at some point in your digital transformation, you will notice a shift from the first to the second category. This will be an indication that your digital transformation (at least as it pertains to mobile) is entering its fourth phase. Companies that don't make a point to distinguish between these two categories of mobile initiatives may not be able to sense their progress from phase to phase nearly as well.

3. Split your mobile strategy into *external* and *internal* initiatives.

Think of your mobile ecosystem in terms of being customer-facing *and* employee-facing. In this chapter, we have focused almost exclusively on customer-facing mobile, but don't forget to think about how mobility might enhance and improve your company's internal processes. (For every customer pain-point, there is an employee pain-point. Find them all.) Some questions to get you started:

- How can we use mobile technologies to solve some of our existing employee pain-points?
- How can we use mobile technologies to reduce operational friction?
- How can we use mobile technologies to improve internal collaboration?
- How can we use mobile technologies to manage projects and campaigns better?
- How can we use mobile technologies to better manage our logistics?
- How can we use mobile technologies to improve productivity?
- How can we use mobile technologies to manage an increasingly mobile and offsite workforce?

In short, the question is: How can we leverage mobile technologies to build a better, faster, more agile company?

The good news is that everything you need to get started is right here in this chapter. The slightly *less* good news is that it's going to take work to bridge the gap between opportunity and results, but you are probably already used to that.

CHAPTER 12:

BIG DATA SOLVES
BIG BUSINESS PROBLEMS

We can't talk about digital transformation without discussing "big data." Let's start with the basics: What exactly is big data? (And what makes it so "big" anyway?) We all know that data are information. At its most granular, data can be precise: the age of a customer, the gender of a shopper, the location of a web page visitor, the number of clicks on an ad in the last hour, what type of operating system someone was using to view your mobile site, and so on. When we talk about data, we talk about bits of information. These bits of information can be batched into sets, and these sets can grow into massive buckets of data that, without databases and spreadsheets and computing power, it would be difficult to make any sense of in a timely or effective manner. Big data, in the simplest sense of the term, refers to massive data sets.

At no other time in history have organizations been able to collect so much information on pretty much whatever they want so fast and cost effectively - Information on sales, market trends, in-store traffic, website visitors... anything you want to know that can help you make better business decisions or optimize a process or dial-in your marketing, you can find out quickly and without having to send out surveys or hire a research firm. Data collection at scale is cheap, fast and accessible to businesses, regardless of their size. You don't even need an expensive or complicated IT infrastructure to access it. Both the data and data collection tools live out there, in the cloud.

WHETHER YOU KNOW IT OR NOT, YOU ARE ALREADY FAMILIAR WITH HOW BIG DATA WORKS.

If you have ever used a retailer's discount (or membership) card, you probably understand that your card is a tool used by that retailer to track your transactional behaviors. First, applying for the card provides the retailer with your name, address, phone number, email, and perhaps other bits of information about you, like your age, gender and family status. Every time you use that card to shop, your transactions are captured and logged. Computers immediately analyze your shopping behaviors and preferences, and a more detailed profile of you starts to emerge. Based on your purchases, someone in your house is vegetarian. You own a dog, the small kind. You own a bird too. You have children under the age of 10. You never use coupons. You prefer to shop on your way home from work or from picking up the kids at school. Based on your address and your propensity to buy premium brands, your income bracket falls somewhere above $175,000 a year. This is why they call it "big data" and why it is so pervasive in the business discussion today.

Think about the kind of data that your bank or credit card company can access. Instead of your behaviors regarding one retailer, the data looks at your behavior everywhere. How often do you visit Starbucks? How often do you travel for work? Where do you like to go on vacation and how much money you spend on hotels, food and souvenirs? Do you fly economy of first class? Your entire life is analyzed based on your purchasing decisions, on how you spend your money, where you spend it and how much you spend. Computers always are working in the background, creating a profile that tells the story of you and your tastes and habits, and predicts your future behaviors.

Now add your digital footprint into the mix. How much time do you spend on your computer vs. your phone? What topics and keywords do you search for online? What ads do you click on? Where do you shop online? *How* do you shop online? How much do you spend online any given month, and what types of products and services do you buy? What apps do you have on your phone, and how often do you use them? Are you a gamer? Are you an athlete? Are you a news hound? Do you spend more time reading left-leaning or right-leaning news sites?

From Google to Facebook to Amazon to Apple, every click, every swipe, every download, every like, and every share helps tell the story of you. Just like your transactions at that retailer we talked about earlier, every action is tracked, logged, categorized, and plugged into an algorithm that creates an ever more specific behavioral profile of *you*.

Imagine how much data can be collected from just one person in 12 months... five years... 10 years. Imagine how granular that data can get. You are talking about stacks and stacks of data points, right? In the old days, this would represent entire boxes of folders, the thick kind. Visualize that for a second, boxes and folders on a shelf somewhere, containing all of your information, all of your data. Now imagine the same for a thousand people. How many warehouses would you need to store all of that? How about a million people? How about 500 million? How about four billion? That's big data. Billions of bits of it collected every second. Obviously, there are no boxes or folders and the warehouses are in the form of data centers. The shelves and boxes are servers. The folders are virtual. All of that data is stored digitally now, organized by software, analyzed by increasingly smart computers that look for patterns and automatically generate predictive models that companies can then use to target customers and prospective customers with the right kinds of offers at precisely the right time.

THE REVOLUTION IN DATA COLLECTION, AGGREGATION, ANALYSIS, AND APPLICATION

There are five pieces to the big data puzzle: collection, aggregation, distribution, analysis, and application. We are going to focus on just three: collection, analysis and application (or rather, the application of insights).

The collection part is the most complicated. It takes a lot of work to collect the data, teach computers to make order out of chaos (aggregation) and to connect one data set to another (distribution). The more digital human activities and transactions are, the easier it gets for computers to do this sort of work, but this is still the hard part. Collection, aggregation and distribution are where the heavy lifting is.

The analysis and application parts are much simpler. Once you know that Joe only makes $50,000 per year and isn't a frivolous spender, you know that he probably isn't a prime candidate for luxury brand ads. (Joe probably isn't going to buy a brand new $75,000 car this quarter, for instance, so why waste money trying to sell him one?) He probably isn't interested in investing in a timeshare either, or buying a Rolex or vacationing in Monaco later this year. He may, however, be interested in 20 percent off his next haircut and a BOGO coupon from his favorite retailer.

His behavioral profile and the predictive modeling that comes from it can allow advertisers to target Joe with the right ads. (Or, if you want to look at it from an advertiser's point of view, it allows advertisers to identify and connect with an ideal, specific audience for specific offers that best match their wants and needs.) When you understand the impact this has on how media buying was handled in 2010 versus how it will be handled in 2020, 2030 and 2040, you start to see how important this is to companies looking to get the most ROI out of their marketing. Big data isn't just revolutionizing our access to market insights and business intelligence, it also is turning a slow and imperfect process of making gut feeling decisions regarding spend, targeting and messaging into a precise, mathematically-sound science anchored in data, measurement and predictive modeling. (Translation: Companies that embrace big data make better decisions, make them faster and enjoy higher ROI on their marketing spend.)

Big data also helps companies fine tune their audience targeting and optimize their outcomes. They can monitor sales, social channel engagement, company mentions, visits to a website, views of a video, and clicks on an ad in real time. (The ability to create rich real-time performance dashboards has given rise to virtual digital command centers from which product managers, PR departments, customer support teams, and sales managers can gauge the impact of a campaign, product launch or press release, for instance.) Increasingly, these dashboards can live on a tablet or a phone, allowing managers to monitor any number of metrics and insights from anywhere and at any time. This is the sort of access to intelligence that marketers would have killed for (figuratively speaking) just a few years ago.

To get a sense for how much of a game changer this is, imagine if you could travel back in time just 10 years with the kind of data and campaign dashboard available to us today. How much of an advantage would you have over your competitors? How unfair would that advantage be? While they were still struggling to understand how to dedicate resources and where to spend marketing dollars, you would be targeting the right customers with the right offers on the right channels at the right time and doing it at a fraction of what your competitors spent to find out what worked and what didn't.

Now flip that time travel script and travel 10 years forward. Which company do you want to be then? Do you want to be the company with the best data and the best insights or the one still struggling with ineffective targeting and low marketing ROI? Do you want to be the company that can take fast, accurate action on emerging market opportunities or the one that still struggles with strategy, velocity and accuracy? Do you want to be the company that optimizes every customer-facing process and anticipates their needs or the one that struggles to understand why 30 percent of their customers never make a fourth purchase? Do you want to be the company that sees an interactive visualization of all of its sales in real time or the one waiting until the end of the week to get a complete sales report? In a way, "big data" is the wrong term for what we are talking about. It's also "big computing" and "real-time insights" and "rich modeling."

But big data doesn't just allow companies to collect seemingly impossible amounts of information and turn it all into useful insights. Big data also helps companies *transform* these insights into actions. Not just ideas for campaigns, but specific micro-targeted *tactical* actions that can be delivered, with minimal effort, on a massive scale.

BIG DATA'S IMPACT ON CUSTOMER EXPERIENCE MOMENTS

What do we mean by "micro-targeted tactical actions?" Think back to our discussion about Disney and the MagicBand bracelets. Park visitors are magically greeted by name whenever they enter a restaurant. Every screen they touch instantly recognizes them and helps them get to their next destination. Even their hotel room remembers who they are. Those are *micro-targeted* (targeting a single customer or customer unit) *tactical* (using specific, specialized resources) *actions* (something done to trigger or drive a *reaction*). A shopping cart that reminds a shopper to buy milk as he passes the dairy aisle because it knows that he just bought a box of breakfast cereal is a micro-targeted tactical action. "Welcome back, Ms. Jones," a lunch-time two-for-one special popping up in your notification tray as you happen to be within walking distance of your favorite pizzeria, and a customized email previewing your favorite apparel brand's upcoming collection are all examples of micro-targeted tactical actions. Unlike mass marketing campaigns, they are *relevant, timely* and *personal*. They don't speak to a vast audience, but to one person, specifically, and often by name. Big data allow companies to do this for thousands, even millions of customers and prospects simultaneously, and this process can be mostly automated and virtually hands-free.

Once you understand the potential, it becomes clear that big data is the key to a company's ability to design *and* scale personalized customer care. This is the answer to two of our original quandaries:

1. In the experience economy, how can brands create remarkable, even magical, experiences for customers?
2. In the experience economy, how can brands scale remarkable, even magical, experiences?

Big data are the key to both of these questions. It is only natural that we now turn those questions into more actionable versions, given the work you are putting into creating a roadmap for digital transformation.

1. How can we leverage big data to create remarkable experiences for our customers?
2. How can we use big data to scale these experiences?

If these questions, like "how can we use big data to build a better company?" seem too macro, here are some somewhat more targeted questions you should work on answering with your department heads and/or management team:

- How can big data help us make better IT, marketing, messaging, and other business decisions?
- How can big data help us monitor and measure performance better?
- How can big data help us make the most out of our marketing dollars?
- How can big data help make our marketing less annoying and more effective?
- How can big data help us build better dashboards for our employees and decision-makers?
- How can big data help us *identify* problems faster?
- How can big data help us *solve* these problems faster?
- How can big data help us identify and understand opportunities better?
- How can big data help us improve outcomes (marketing, sales, customer acquisition, customer retention, customer loyalty, product design, pricing, etc.)?
- How can big data help us improve productivity?
- How can big data help us hire better?

- How can big data help us transition from "where were our customers a month ago?" to "where were our customers an hour ago" to "where are our customers right now?" to "where will our customers be an hour from now?"

We don't want to go quite so far as to suggest that the questions you ask of big data turn into a general "what could a magical crystal ball actually do for us," but, given the types of insights that big data (especially combined with artificial intelligence) already can provide, it might not be as silly an exercise as you might think. Working backward from an ideal "crystal ball" model to what big data can do for your company may actually be easier and faster than working forward from your company's current data mining capabilities.

When it comes to this particular aspect of your digital transformation, it actually pays to think big and dream big, not because dreaming big is good for morale, but because when it comes to this particular piece of the technology puzzle, the gap between fantasy and reality happens to be closing quickly.

CHAPTER 13:

THE CLOUD AS A BUSINESS ENABLER

"Cloud" is a brilliant term when you think about it. It's pretty. It's poetic. It's as non-IT as a word can possibly be. And yet, "cloud" is pretty much synonymous with IT. Whether you are talking about *the* cloud, or clouds (plural), unless you are looking up at the sky and discussing your weekend or your team's upcoming golf tournament, the term, whenever uttered in a business context, refers to modern IT. But, what is the cloud anyway? It's complicated, but basically it is an ecosystem of networked computers that can provide everything you would expect an IT department to, but at scale, as a service via the web. It's a bit like a power or water utility, but for IT.

Why is the cloud important? To answer that question, you have to go back a few years and look at how IT used to work, or rather how limited and boxed-in IT was. Most IT investments (infrastructure/hardware investments, *computing power* investments, *data storage* investments, software investments, expertise, etc.) were all in-house. You needed your own servers to store your data in-house. It was expensive and complicated, which meant that small- and medium-sized businesses couldn't compete technologically with larger, better funded companies. Another problem with the old IT model was that investments in what we now refer to as "legacy" systems were exactly that — investments in *legacy* systems. They were more relevant to the past than the present, let alone the future. These servers and computers were reliable, but they weren't particularly adaptable to change. By the time companies pulled the trigger on their new front-heavy technology investment, they already were playing yesterday's game instead of tomorrow's, and that doesn't exactly help anyone drive innovation and digital transformation.

An additional problem with the old IT model was that, computing capacity was limited to whatever your IT infrastructure could handle. If you suddenly needed to double your overall capacity, you couldn't. You were stuck with what you had.

Fast forward to today's "cloud." The cloud takes IT out of the box it was stuck in for decades. Among other things, cloud computing offers access to on-demand computing capacity and potentially unlimited data storage. This means that companies of any size can now scale their IT capacity at will.

Back to the water utility example we used at the start of the chapter, switching from in-house legacy systems to the cloud is a lot like going from having to dig your own well in your back yard and wrestling with a pump that isn't getting any younger to being able to turn on a tap anywhere in your house and access water from a service that handles all of its maintenance and upgrades for you. It's cheaper, virtually hassle-free and a lot more efficient.

Unless you're a Fortune 500 juggernaut with a quasi-unlimited IT budget, your in-house IT department never will be agile enough to provide you with all of the computing power, data storage and access to high performance software you need to effectively pull off a digital transformation of any consequence. Leveraging the cloud, however, makes it possible. Even if you are one of those Fortune 500 companies, it makes sense to leverage the cloud as well.

DOES THIS MEAN THAT OUR IT DEPARTMENT IS OBSOLETE?

We aren't suggesting that your company shut down its IT department and move everything to the cloud. Don't get rid of your internal servers just yet. Cloud services versus legacy IT doesn't have to be an *either/ or* proposition. It can be an *and* proposition. For most companies, it actually makes sense to keep some IT capacity in-house and look to the cloud to fill gaps and build on what is already there. This model is what is usually referred to as *hybrid IT* or *hybridized IT*. It seeks to balance between these two functions and get the most out of both. There is a lot of value to using both.

A hybrid IT model allows you to thoughtfully leverage your IT assets *and* cut costs at the same time. Consider, for example, the impact to your company of a 30-40 percent cost reduction in IT. What would that budget surplus allow you to do?

A hybrid IT model also allows you to determine what parts of your infrastructure you want to keep for easy accessibility. Need to troubleshoot an issue quickly? Keeping critical IT applications in-house keeps them accessible. Likewise, certain cloud-based solutions can be easily managed remotely from a laptop or mobile device. (No more emergency server reboots at 2 a.m. on a Sunday, for instance. Or maybe just fewer of them.) A hybrid IT model allows you to customize your IT infrastructure, not just in terms of cost and capacity, but also modes of access.

WHAT ABOUT RISK?

The beauty of hybrid IT models (as opposed to full-cloud models) is that they help companies mitigate risk, particularly in regard to data security. Keeping proprietary and personal in-house will minimize the threat of a breach. This strategy is especially helpful in industries like healthcare and finance, where the transfer of patient or customer information is commonplace. The same is true of certain types of critical applications.

To determine what should be kept in-house and what can be stored on the cloud, think about using a structured classification system to sort and categorize your data and applications. This, and the use of encryption, should go a long way toward protecting you from data breaches.

RESISTANCE AND COMPETENCE: OVERCOMING IT'S MOST COMMON HURDLES

Since we have already discussed mobile, social business and big data, you already understand the importance of the cloud. Without it, your company most likely won't be able to access, store, process, or analyze much of the data you need to build a truly digital company. Without it, you also can forget about playing in the mobile space and the social business space at all. (It's physically impossible.) Marketing automation, artificial intelligence, the Internet of things, virtualization, e-commerce... none of those things work without the cloud. What this means is that your company's ability to integrate the cloud into its IT universe is vital to the success of its digital transformation.

One of the trickiest aspects of your digital transformation, at least at its inception, is making sure your staff is capable of helping you build the processes and systems you need to make it all happen. Your social business team should know how to build, manage and grow a social business, for instance. Your experience designers should know how to design experiences. From your accounting and customer service departments to your mobile integration and product management teams, everyone should be capable, competent and on point. This also applies to your IT department.

One of the friction points you may run into as you embark on your journey of digital transformation is a certain... *reluctance* by some members of your IT department to make changes to the way they run IT. This may signal that not everyone in your IT department has the know-how to help you transition to a cloud-enabled IT model. Be on the lookout for that. If training is all that is required, that's an easy fix. If training won't do it, you may have some difficult choices to make. At the end of the day, you are running a business. If some elements of your IT department can't or won't help you make your company more competitive, it may be time to replace them with IT professionals who will. Yes, this may seem harsh, but this isn't an area that you can afford to get even 10 percent wrong. Every IT resource in your business ecosystem needs to be 100 percent onboard and capable to help you do this.

BECAUSE OF THE CLOUD, THE ROLE OF IT IS CHANGING.

In the old days of IT, the IT department used to be a little insular. They were the priests of tech, the guardians of arcane knowledge, the keepers of secret keys. They rarely attended line of business (LoB) meetings, didn't interfere much with departmental strategy and only ventured out of their Faraday cage when someone had a technical question or a computer problem they couldn't figure out on their own. This is no longer a viable operational model.

Technology has become so important to every aspect of business today that IT professionals and LoB professionals have to work as partners on pretty much everything. This is a big operational shift, but it doesn't have to be difficult (Besides, you don't have a choice.) Thanks to the cloud, you are going to build a more agile and decentralized IT infrastructure. Doesn't it make sense that your IT department become more agile and decentralized as well?

For starters, move IT out of the IT cave. Assign an IT resource to every LoB. *Marketing* should have its own (probably more than one) IT resource. *Sales* should have its own IT resource as well. Social business and customer service and BI (Business Intelligence) should too. Just like digital agencies increasingly embed resources inside their clients' organizations, IT departments should embed resources inside all key departments. IT's role is to help LoBs a) overcome their specific technical hurdles *and* b) leverage technology to improve their outcomes. IT *cannot* do that if it doesn't understand what the LoBs' objectives are and if it doesn't have eyes on what problems they are trying to solve daily.

Departments need embedded tech experts to help them solve problems and build their own digital capabilities. In turn, these tech experts also must be empowered to act as LoB advocates within the company's IT department. This dynamic, symbiotic relationship between IT and other departments is essential to a company's digital transformation.

The flip side of that operational coin is that LoB professionals, especially in management and decision-making roles, can no longer afford to be IT-illiterate. The partnership we just outlined works both ways. If IT is going to essentially *cross-train* in LoB studies, non-IT resources also have to learn a few things about IT capabilities, tech in general and cloud solutions. This is much easier to accomplish when IT is working side-by-side daily with marketing managers and customer experience designers than when they only meet once a month in a conference room. CMOs and sales managers have to become more IT- and cloud-savvy or they won't be able to do their jobs.

SOME QUICK OPERATIONAL ADVICE FOR LOB MANAGERS

Let's say that your company's IT department hasn't quite bought into the *embedded resource* model or just doesn't have the resources to spare just yet. Let's also assume your IT department still wrestles with the limitations of its own in-house servers. It is running into capacity issues and outages, and they still aren't running the software solutions you need. Your tech roadblocks exist, and you need to find a way through or around them. It's probably time to have a sit-down with your IT management team to discuss your needs and how they intend to address them properly within the next six months. Invite the CFO to that discussion since it cannot end with "budget shortfalls" or "maybe next year" or "we have a plan, and we'll get your needs eventually." If the objection to solving your problem is financial, having the CFO in the room will help. When the objection shifts to IT's limited technical capabilities, the old "we're tied down to the technology we have already invested in," you must reiterate that you aren't tied down to anything. If the "technology you have invested in" (dusty old servers and outdated software solutions) isn't doing the job anymore, move *your* technical needs to the cloud, where you can have access to all the software and capacity you need on demand. Be prepared to make your cost-benefit argument to the CFO and to call on the IT department to help you find and deploy the cloud-based solutions you need. If IT still won't do it, get the funding to take care of it yourself. It won't take long for IT to adjust after that.

SUMMARY

1. The cloud is a digital and technical force-multiplier for businesses. It allows IT departments to build agile on-demand technical capacity at a fraction of the cost of traditional IT.

2. The cloud provides companies with virtually unlimited computing capacity, scale and speed with minimal investment and no significant upfront risk.

3. The cloud is the technical foundation upon which your company's digital transformation must be built. It can't be done properly without it.

4. To remain relevant to companies committed to their digital transformation, IT must reinvent its value proposition inside these organizations, and move from *guardians of an arcane and complicated technology infrastructure*, to *internal centers for the agile deployment of technology solutions* that every LoB wants to partner with.

5. IT must to shift from being the department of "no, we can't" to the department of "yes we can."

6. IT must become more operational, move into the day-to-day of LoBs and get more involved with technology enablement, planning and tactical support at the departmental level.

If your access to cloud solutions finally make this IT shift possible, your digital transformation makes it *necessary*. Partner with your IT department and start looking at how it too will have to adapt to change for cloud adoption. Forward-thinking IT managers will see this as an opportunity to transform IT into an indispensible powerhouse and will jump at the opportunity to help propel their department forward. Others may resist, but, ultimately, progress waits for no one.

CHAPTER 14:

OTHER KEY TECHNOLOGY TRENDS

In many ways, our vision of the future today isn't so different from the vision of the future that permeated our culture 50 or 100 years ago. Consider futurist predictions from the early 20th century, which predicted flying mailmen, handheld wireless video telephones, mass transit systems, and flying cars. When we look back on how the people of that era imagined what these technological marvels would look like, their ideas seem dated and charmingly retro to us, but they also are wonderfully close to the truth.

Consider one of the most fantastical of those predictions — flying mailmen. Obviously, mail delivery isn't done from the saddle of a flying machine, but consider what companies like Amazon have been experimenting with recently — flying delivery drones. The first man-carrying drone was introduced at the Consumer Electronics Show (CES) in early 2016. More ubiquitous now are the handheld, wireless video telephones. Our smartphones made that prediction come true. Of course, we're still waiting on flying cars to become mainstream, but several designs have been tested successfully, so we have reached that milestone. For the time being, self-driving cars seem to be where futurist locomotion is headed, at least at scale. The point is that almost every device and technological marvel dreamed up a century or more ago was invented. Our imagination does drive progress and innovation.

In the post World War II era, for instance, many of the "future" technologies dreamed up by contemporaries of HG Wells and Jules Verne were adapted to practical mass-market products, most of which centered around the home and the office, including:

- Automatic laundry machines,
- Automatic ovens,
- Automatic dishwashers,
- Electric bread makers, and
- Electric food mixers.

They seem commonplace to us now, but, when they were first introduced, they were the tip of the technological spear, modern marvels and status symbols. Seventy years from now, what popular technologies will our descendants find cute and quaint? Perhaps:

- Smart appliances?
- Smart homes?
- Fitness wearables?
- Social Media?
- Smartphones?
- Smart TVs?
- Tablets?
- Self-driving cars?

Although innovation itself isn't linear, there is an almost a linear quality to the commercialization of technological progress. Technology trends are fairly predictable, in the short *and* the long term. This means that good science fiction and "futurism" aren't prophetic. They merely point to the bleachers the way Babe Ruth used to before hitting a home run.

TECHNOLOGIES THAT MAY CHANGE YOUR WORLD IN THE NEXT FIVE TO 10 YEARS

In this chapter, we are going to point you to some of the most important technology trends that you should familiarize yourself with before moving forward with your digital transformation. These are all vertical-agnostic technologies (technologies that aren't limited to a specific industry), so we won't go into things like artificial organs (healthcare) or smart grids (energy). We are focusing on technologies that will help you innovate and build a better, more modern version of your company.

Here is a short list:

- The Internet of Things (IoT),
- Virtualization,
- Virtual reality,
- Augmented and mixed reality, and
- Artificial intelligence (AI) and cognitive computing.

Let's dive a little deeper into each one. Once we're done, we will circle back to digital transformation and discuss how to best incorporate these technologies into your company's future.

1. The Internet of Things (IoT)

Granted, "the internet of things" is not the most elegant taxonomy for connected devices, but it is the accepted one. Wikipedia will tell you that this particular branch of the technology tree refers to "the network of physical objects (devices, vehicles, buildings and other items embedded with electronics, software, sensors, and network connectivity) that enables these objects to collect and exchange data." As that is as good a definition as any, let's keep things simple and stick to that.

What is the importance of IoT? From a commercial standpoint, and looking at experience design, IoT is one of the most exciting opportunities available to companies today. Remember Disney's MagicBand? That is a massive IoT play. Disney combined Big Data, a hybrid IT/cloud model and electronic bracelets to turn data collection into data processing, and data processing into the crafting of magical and personalized experiences.

Now consider how a home appliance company might be able to revolutionize homeowner experience design by using IoT technology to connect its products to the web, learning computers or an app that lives on their owners' phones. Everything in a house, from the thermostat to the dishwasher, could become smarter, better and more fun to use. Imagine a refrigerator that monitors its own contents, generates shopping lists, and sends them right to your phone so you never again forget to buy milk, mayonnaise or lettuce. Imagine a kitchen whose cupboards you can check from your phone to find out, while you are at the store, if you need to buy bread, chips or soda.

IoT technology is already everywhere, from smart TVs and smartphones to wearables. Athletes use IoT technology to monitor performance. Medical professionals use IoT technology to monitor patients. Military and police units use IoT technology to keep tabs on where their people are. IoT technology essentially builds new layers of utility into existing systems, but the value doesn't have to stop there. Author David Rose refers to the next generation of IoT devices as "enchanted objects. [36]" These are IoT devices that don't just provide valuable new utility. By virtue of creating cool, fun, delightful, and seemingly magical experiences, they *enchant* users. Part of their value is tied to the experience they help create. Examples of enchanted objects are self-parking cars (and increasingly self-driving cars), Amazon's voice-activated *Echo* smart speaker and emotive robot companions.

What are opportunities for your company? Well, it depends. Luxury resorts won't use IoT technology the way that hospitals will, for instance. Schools won't use IoT technology the same way that toymakers will. Don't worry though, we will get to how to figure out how to make this and other technologies fit into your business universe.

2. Virtualization

Virtualization is the creation of a *virtual* version of something, such as a product, a mechanical part or a system. Most products today, from athletic shoes to sports cars, are designed virtually, through the use of 3D virtualization software. Increasingly, the actual testing of prototypes (heat, drop, crash, and load tests) also takes place virtually. Virtualization software has become so advanced that materials themselves, right down to their molecular structure, can be virtualized. This allows researchers to develop and test medical implants and experimental drugs virtually without having to risk the lives of living test subjects, and with an equal (if not greater) degree of control and accuracy. Computing power also allows designers and data analysts to push virtualization in the other direction and go big. Virtualization can model and test infinitely complex systems like power grids, global weather patterns, water usage in drought-afflicted regions, and global financial systems.

Virtualization is essentially a cost-effective way of quickly developing and testing ideas, no matter how small, large or complex. Once the realm of design engineers, virtualization is becoming far more mainstream, allowing companies to accelerate innovation while minimizing risk. It

---

[36]Rose, D. (2015). *Enchanted objects: Innovation, design, and the future of technology.* New York, NY: Scribner.

also can be used in "what if?" data modeling, multilayered marketing campaign design and virtual retail experience design, which should be lighting a few figurative light bulbs right about now. If your interest lies more with manufacturing and logistics, virtualization can help you optimize production, reinvent the way you think of inventory and shipping, and coordinate millions of deliveries at a glance.

One particularly fascinating development in virtualization technology is its growing co-creation applications. For instance, if you visit a car manufacturer's website, chances are that at some point in your browsing journey, you will be given the option to customize the car you are looking at. You will be able to change its color, add features, modify the interior, etc. This is an example of virtualization technology applied to co-creation and retail. The website is generating a virtual photorealistic version of the vehicle and letting you see how it will look with all of your personalized customizations.

Increasingly, this type of experience is bleeding into retail experiences. For instance, fashion brands are experimenting with custom design virtualization of shoes, shirts, pants, messenger bags, electronics, accessories, etc. These personalized design experiences also can be moved in-store with the use of digital stations where shoppers can design their own versions of the items they are interested in, then order them onsite. On the logistics side, virtualization is used to design, test and optimize resource allocation, schedules, delivery fleets, and so on.

3. Virtual reality (VR)

Virtual reality refers to a computer-generated simulation of a three-dimensional environment that usually can be interacted with by users through electronic devices like special goggles, special gloves and other objects containing special sensors. For all its coolness and promise, virtual reality is still in its relative infancy and has been plagued with false starts, near misses, and a general sense that there is still a long way to go before we can expect to seamlessly slip in and out of flawless virtual worlds. Having said that, VR is a big play in the tech world and loads of companies are investing in its development.

What kinds of applications seem relevant in the near future (besides gaming)? Let's look at three:

- **3D virtualization.** We just talked about virtualization in its traditional format — screens, laptops, tablets, displays... essentially flat space.

With VR technology, designers can go inside their virtualizations and experience them from a different perspective. Architects can "walk" through their buildings. Vehicle designers can "drive" their cars and fly their planes, and engineers can manipulate parts and drawings faster and more intuitively than they would using a screen, mouse and keyboard. Interacting with their virtualizations in fully rendered 3D environments takes virtualization to a whole new level of performance.

- **Training and education.** There's a reason why pilots learn how to fly on flight simulators before getting inside a real cockpit. While professional flight simulators were once bulky and ridiculously expensive, VR can help replace some of the more costly aspects of building and maintain flight simulators. It also can help scale training, expand the number of environments and situations used in training and bring technical specificity into training that was not possible before. This doesn't just apply to pilots and flight simulators, by the way. Any type of technical training can be virtualized, from teaching mechanics how to work on certain types of engines to teaching surgeons how to remove a gall bladder.

- **Remote control.** The old way of flying a drone was through a handheld control unit with joysticks and wheels, and by keeping your eyes on where the drone was. The new way of flying a drone is through the use of VR goggles, linked to one or more cameras mounted on the drone itself. VR technology puts the pilot "in the driver's seat" so he or she can fly the drone with more accuracy. Applications for remote-control VR likely will expand to other types of vehicles (trains, planes, cruise ships, police interceptors, combat vehicles, etc.) and robots (search and rescue, mining, diving, and so on). In healthcare, one of the plays with VR is to allow a surgeon standing in, say, Toronto, Canada, to operate remotely on a patient in, say, Cairo, Egypt.

Virtual reality has applications that reach far beyond the world of gaming and entertainment, so don't sell it short or mistake it for a fad. Tech companies will never stop working on VR, which tells you that it will increasingly be part of our lives.

4. Augmented and mixed reality

Augmented reality (AR) is a technology that superimposes a computer-generated image onto a user's view of the real world by way of a digital screen. By combining reality and virtual objects, AR creates a hybrid or composite view. Usually, AR is accomplished by projecting virtual images onto a phone or other mobile screen while the screen happens to be showing an image captured by the device's camera.

Among the existing uses for AR are GPS navigation, helping amateur chefs learn recipes, helping excavation crews visualize the location of pipelines in the area where they are about to dig, and helping DIYers do pretty much anything from gardening to auto repair. A museum could also easily use AR to add layers of interactivity to a tour. Hold up your phone to discover interactive information bubbles and even find yourself interviewing a portrait or George Washington or statue of Julius Caesar.

Mixed reality (MR) is the merging of real world and virtual worlds to produce a new environment where physical and digital objects can co-exist and interact. This falls halfway between VR and AR. Basically, think of MR as AR with VR goggles. Instead of interacting with a composite image, you interact with a composite environment.

A tourism company in New Orleans, for example, might use MR to augment a haunted tour of the French Quarter. Participants equipped with special goggles could see ghosts and creepy shadows, turning the tour into a much more interactive and memorable experience than simply walking around listening to stories.

AR and MR are ideal technologies to enhance and augment customer experiences. Retail is an obvious environment for AR. Allowing shoppers to hold up their phones or devices to uncover special offers hiding throughout a store would add a new layer to their shopping experience. Giving them the option to see "their" price hovering virtually over an item (as opposed to the price everyone else sees) also might prompt them to purchase items they wouldn't otherwise. Retailers also are experimenting with "magic mirrors," which project a virtual image of a garment they browsed onto their reflection. (No need to waste time going into a fitting room to see what you would look like wearing it.) Internally, Mixed Reality might lead to the next evolution in conference calls, interactive presentations and collaboration. Imagine a product design team's ability to present its progress on a new product design by allowing everyone in the meeting (whether they are physically in the same conference room or sitting in their office a continent away) to manipulate a photorealistic 3D virtual prototype which, much like a hologram, would appear in front of them. Think about the impact this would have on architectural design, retail design, and logistics and planning alone. Imagine how much easier collaboration, especially remote (mobile) collaboration, would be when project teams can interact with each other and their projects in this way instead of just reading emails and opening two-dimensional files on their computers.

5. Artificial intelligence (AI) and cognitive computing

We mentioned artificial intelligence (AI) a lot in previous chapters, so let's dive into it a little deeper now. AI is a type of computer system that performs tasks we normally associate with human intelligence.

Cognitive computing refers to the simulation of human thought processes by a computer system. It usually involves self-learning, intuitive data mining, pattern recognition, and natural language processing to mimic the way the human brain works.

Although there is a difference between AI and cognitive computing, cognitive computing is generally a function (a subset, if you will) of AI. So when we talk about AI in this book, we tend also to be referencing cognitive computing.

Applications for cognitive computing and AI are so wide-reaching that we could easily write a dozen books on the subject. Right now, let's focus on how both fit into your digital transformation and the world in which your customers live. First, consider the four key capabilities of cognitive computing we just mentioned:

1. Self-learning,
2. Intuitive data mining,
3. Pattern recognition, and
4. Natural language processing.

These computers are capable of learning on their own. They naturally look for hidden patterns in data. They can be made to look for ways of mining and organizing data that will best serve user needs, and can be interacted with using natural language rather than complex programming.

Now combine these capabilities with big data and cloud computing and you have are intelligent, intuitive supercomputers that can sift through massive amounts of data in real time, interpret it for you, and identify patterns and opportunities you hadn't imagined. Not only that, but this can be delivered at scale, to any company anywhere, like any other digital service.

The combined computing, data management, analytical, virtualization, and modeling power that was once the staple of science-fiction novels and movies is now real. For instance, IBM's mix of cognitive computing, cloud and big data management has turned Watson, its famous cognitive-computer (and Jeopardy champion), into a scalable juggernaut of potential for pretty much every professional you can think of — city planners, medical researchers, astronomers, physicists, legal scholars, marketers, geostrategists, screenwriters, warehouse designers, intelligence services, climatologists, economists, designers, and even chefs. (Watson is developing his own recipes now.)

Dassault Systemes, whose products include the ubiquitous design engineering must-have *Solidworks*, has leveraged virtualization, cloud and cognitive computing to beef up its portfolio of products and services so that it can deliver the types of solutions that what we talked about throughout this book — multiphysics modeling and simulation, consumer experience modeling, unified data discovery and management, collaboration platforms for innovation teams, supply-chain optimization, intelligence dashboard personalization, real-time social analytics, decision-support, and more, at scale, and deliverable anywhere in the world.

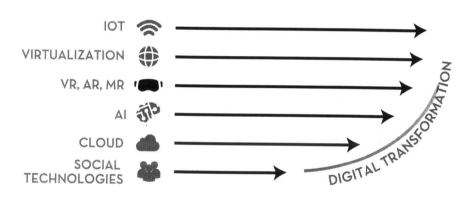

Fig. 14.1: **How New Technologies Feed Digital Transformation**

TIP: THE MORE YOU COMBINE TECHNOLOGIES, THE MORE THEY CAN ACHIEVE

The key here, as you may have guessed, isn't so much to figure out how a single new technology might help your business, but how several of them combined, especially combined with technologies and systems you are already using, can multiply your capabilities, efficiency and potential.

In other words, don't just stop at asking how virtualization might help your company design products or retail spaces better. That's a good start, but it is far too insular and limited. Instead, ask how virtualization, combined with big data, IoT, cloud, and social channel intelligence, might help you identify product features you hadn't thought of but that your customers already have, or how it may help you improve retail experiences by analyzing, for instance, traffic patterns inside your stores, figure out whether or not you should place more mirrors throughout the space (and if so, where), and how to improve shoppers' checkout experience by making the lines shorter (or eliminating them altogether).

We obviously are just scratching the surface here, but you get the picture. Smart, self-teaching computers, plus cost-effective, universally embeddable data-collection devices and sensors, plus oceans of discoverable data, plus fast, intuitive, scalable data analysis and pattern recognition, plus frictionless collaboration, plus customizable dashboards equals innovation enablement as a service.

The point of a digital transformation isn't just to develop a social media strategy and look into how mobile can help reach your customers better. It goes much further than that and runs far deeper too.

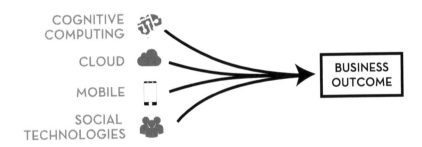

Fig. 14.2: **Combine New Technologies to Deliver Outcomes**

BREAKING DOWN THE EMERGING TECHNOLOGY ANALYSIS DOWN TO A SIMPLE PROCESS

Monitoring emerging technologies is an essential component of any company's ability to adapt to change. Whether your company is still in a reactive mode (defense) or a proactive mode (offense), staying abreast of innovation and new technologies can mean the difference between being in business two years from now or not. Is there a process though? The answer is yes, and that process is predictably simple.

For starters, every company should build innovation discovery into its business model. We are talking about a deliberate process of search, discovery, analysis, and discussion. You will recall our earlier discussion around *ideathons*. This is a similar process in which instead of coming up with ideas, LoB managers and executives are tasked with a) keeping an eye on new technologies *and* inspired uses for these technologies, and b) presenting their findings and observations to a group tasked by management with identifying technology opportunities. These groups can be clustered throughout the organization or centralized, depending on the organization's capabilities and needs. What matters is that this function be built, maintained and taken seriously by decision-makers. A lot obviously depends on it.

The questions that must be answered are fairly simple:

- What emerging technologies and/or market trends should we be aware of? (Make a list.)
- How could we leverage each of these individually to solve a problem, improve a system or disrupt our market?
- How might a competitor use each to disrupt our market or industry ahead of us?
- What sort of ripple effect could each one of them create in our market?
- How could they be combined to help us solve a problem, improve a system or disrupt our market?
- How might a competitor combine them to disrupt our market or industry ahead of us?

Diving a little deeper into the process, you may want to create two different audits: a *direct impact* audit and an *indirect impact* audit.

THE DIRECT IMPACT AUDIT

Focus on what *direct* impact each of these technologies might have on your business, ask:

- How might we leverage this tech to solve a problem for one of our teams?
- How might we leverage this tech to solve a problem for customers?
- How might we leverage this tech to improve an imperfect system?
- How might we leverage this tech to create a new service?
- How might we leverage this tech to penetrate a new market?

Going down our list, we would quickly start to see that *big data* would solve a number of problems for several of our teams. For instance, better, faster and more useful market insights *before* launching a new product development project, and better, faster and more useful market insights for the marketing team once the marketing campaign for that product begins. Net positives: Better intelligence, faster delivery of that intelligence and significantly improved ability to make better decisions based on that intelligence.

Cognitive computing, applied to data analysis and market insights, also could create and test virtual marketing models and scenarios, then predict which ones are most likely to yield the best results. This would eliminate a lot of unnecessary trial and error, shorten project timelines and significantly improve outcomes. (Remember that velocity is a key component of success. If succeeding faster means succeeding faster and failing faster, then succeeding faster, one of the most key traits of successful companies is having the ability to move forward faster. One of the many key advantages of incorporating artificial intelligence into both *big data* analysis and predictive modeling is *velocity*.)

How smart devices fit into a business model is a little less universal than *big data* and *AI*, but the insight process is the same. Perhaps you can use it internally to optimize energy needs in a green office building or modify subtle environmental settings to help boost productivity later in the day. Externally, perhaps some of your products and services could be enhanced or augmented by sensors, connectivity, feedback, and/or some degree of *AI* or data collection. Whatever your product is, sensor technology and the ability to connect any product to cloud-based software have become so cheap that you can bring new utility into that product's value equation. B2B, B2C, B2G... none of that matters anymore. What matters is a single question: How can I use this tech to bring more value to this product or service?

Remember how all of this started:

- How can our company remain competitive and survive? (defense)
- How can our company gain and maintain an advantage over its competitors? (offense)

Feel free to elaborate and think bigger by asking:

- How can we use these technologies to completely redefine a product category?
- How can we use these technologies to become the only relevant player for this product category?
- How can we use these technologies to make all of our competitors in this product category obsolete by this time next year?

This is the right mindset, and from this mindset emerges the process itself. A constant search for new technologies and trends that could help you change the game for a product, service or industry, then leveraging it as fast and aggressively as possible to make the most of that advantage.

THE INDIRECT IMPACT AUDIT

The indirect impact audit is an exercise in which you and your team consider all of the ways that a new technology or trend might impact you by way of your market. Essentially, it is an exercise in thinking about the possible ripple effects of that change.

This should not be limited to a one-time meeting or a quarterly review. It must be part of a continuous process of observation, analysis and discussion, embedded in all strategy and market insights discussions. Most highly innovative companies conduct formal reviews of new tech and market trends weekly, and discuss them informally on a daily basis.

Imagine, for instance, if Blockbuster had kept a better eye on the rise of video downloads and had a formal weekly internal mechanism in place to discuss what it meant to their model down the road. Imagine if the folks at Blackberry had kept a better eye on what Apple was working on, not just in terms of touch-screen technology and hardware, but also its app ecosystem and third-party functionality. Imagine how different a lot of failed or struggling businesses might be today if they had built in an internal mechanism to *proactively* identify opportunities and threats (direct *and* indirect) and had discussed them *with purpose* on an ongoing basis.

Three shining examples of this kind of mindset are Starbucks, Dell and the Ford Motor Company. They were among the first major U.S. companies to identify the rise in popularity of social media as an opportunity to augment their brand relevance, reach more customers and more effectively market to an entirely new generation of consumers. While most other brands were "starting to look into Facebook and Twitter," they already were building a massive followings, creating and sharing content with them, and using channels like Twitter to increase conversions and drive sales.

Lucky guess or calculated market test? Calculated market test. First, the initial "hunch" that pointed these companies toward social channels wasn't just a lucky guess. It was driven by a mechanism focused on identifying new opportunities. By observing these new channels and looking at adoption and user data, early movers in the social media space were able to quantify market behaviors and create forward-looking models. What did these models indicate? Large-scale adoption at a rapid rate. What did this mean? Mapping their market's attention and media consumption, it meant that time spent on social channels was catching up to (and in some cases overtaking) other forms of media (like print media). The conclusion: If attention was shifting from medium A to medium B, both ad spend and marketing dollars also needed to shift from medium A to medium B.

These companies didn't reboot their entire marketing ecosystems overnight on a wild bet. They started by investing a small amount of money and resources to test these new channels , and, over time, grew these market tests into progressively bigger and more sophisticated programs. While scores of other companies waited and stumbled for years to leverage social media properly, these pioneers were able to establish themselves and build successful programs there quickly and cost-effectively. What made them successful? The right mindset, the right processes, and the ability to execute with velocity and agility.

Tip: You don't have to work as hard to sell a revolutionary new idea to executives if they already tasked you with identifying such opportunities for them.
Unfortunately far too many companies *still* operate under a passive model in which new technologies and trends are treated as mere line items during monthly and quarterly meetings. Ripple effects are

therefore barely touched on until they begin to take effect, and, by then, it may be too late. The *idea* of a mindset might be there, but not the mindset itself. Absent the right mindset, the processes that grow out of it, and the subsequent ability to execute on a market test or new idea, discussions and meetings rarely turn into anything concrete, and digital transformation remains stalled and rudderless.

Creating this discovery, analysis and review process within the scope of a digital transformation initiative improves a company's ability to anticipate change and make necessary course corrections. All that remains beyond that is the creation of a path to adoption and deployment, which falls squarely in the realm of digital transformation.

CHAPTER 15:

SOME THOUGHTS ABOUT GOALS, TARGETS AND MEASUREMENT

Measuring success during a digital transformation journey can seem a bit complicated, but once you get the hang of it, it will become as natural to your organization as any other current type of measurement. What is important early on is to get organized, breaking down measurement into categories and priorities. Generally speaking, the three major categories of measurement you will focus on are:

1. Net business metrics that you already pay attention to (sales, ROI, web traffic, etc.).
2. Deltas (changes) in metrics directly attributable to your digital transformation.
3. Adoption and deployment targets (whether or not you are hitting your digital transformation milestones on schedule and on budget, for example).

The first part is easy. Even though a lot is changing throughout your company, sales are sales, website traffic is still website traffic, impressions are still impressions, and customer retention is still customer retention. What you were measuring a year ago still is likely to be important to measure moving forward. In fact, it is vital that you continue to track the progress of every measurable aspect of your business's performance as any change in your pre-digital transformation baseline (or trending) will identify areas impact by its success or failure.

To make this monitoring and analysis process easier, consider moving all of your business metrics to an analytics dashboard and using cognitive computing software to identify patterns of success, stagnation and failure. Also look for trends that may be accelerating or slowing down and shifts you might have otherwise missed. (For instance, your net sales may remain constant at 9 percent YoY growth, but your online retail channel may be growing by 20 percent YoY against your brick-and-mortar retail channel. Using intuitive dashboards will help you make better sense of your business metrics and should help you make fast, smart decisions about where to allocate resources and how.

The second category of metrics you should focus on pertains to those you intended to impact directly or indirectly through the deployment of a new technology or process. For instance, if one of the outcomes driving a particular aspect of your digital transformation is improved customer experiences in your retail stores, create a specific dashboard that focuses on these metrics. These measurements might include results from overall customer satisfaction surveys, analysis of social media mentions within 24 hours of a purchase or shopping experience, a noticeable change in the frequency of customer visits or the average amount of their purchases, or it might even use cameras and sensors to analyze customer's facial expressions and behaviors as they go through various stages of their shopping journey, particularly toward the end, as they prepare to make a purchase, then leave the store (smiles are good; frowns are bad).

If your objective was less vague than "improve" or "accelerate," and actually set a target, measure your actual outcome against the target you set. For example, let's say that one of your technology deployment projects was meant to accelerate product development by 20 percent. Six months into deployment, test that. Has it worked? On average, has product development accelerated 20 percent? If the improvement hovers around 11 percent, you have more work to do. If the improvement looks more like 40 percent, bravo, you have exceeded your goal. (Hey, it happens.) The point is that you won't know exactly how effective an investment in a new technology, process or system was unless you actually measure its success against the goals you set for it. Whatever you mean to impact — employee retention, customer engagement, mobile retail sales, warehouse logistics, customer lifecycle value, marketshare, profitability, innovation velocity — build a specific measurement practice (and dashboard) devoted to metrics relevant to it.

The third category of metrics focuses on your change management initiative. Rather than focusing on identifying deltas, and quantifying impact and outcomes, these metrics focus exclusively on whether your organization is on schedule and on budget to hit your digital transformation milestones. Chances are that some initiatives may reach those milestones earlier than expected, while others may fall behind. Without a measurement practice devoted to this aspect of your digital transformation, executives and decision-makers may not be aware of problems quickly enough to do much about them. Creating a monitoring and measurement practice (and dashboard) around these metrics gives managers and decision-makers a real-time view of a project's trajectory against its original roadmap, which gives them the ability to make timely course corrections (assigning additional resources to a project team, replacing an ineffective project manager, sourcing a different technology partner, and so on) as needed.

EMBRACING ALL OF THE LAYERS: CHANGE MANAGEMENT OBJECTIVES VS. LOB OBJECTIVES

Metrics, as they pertain to a digital transformation initiative, are layered. The executive and management team tasked with overseeing the progress and success of the organization's digital transformation has its own layer of metrics to focus on. Likewise, LoB managers have their own metrics to focus on, from sales to customer satisfaction to zero-failure manufacturing. The trick for the executives trying to make sense of it all is to somehow combine all of these layers of interconnected metrics in a way that makes sense.

Ironically, the types of technologies we are talking about integrating into your business ecosystem can give executives and decision-makers the ability to do just that. We suggest you:

- Take all of that data and connect it in a way that makes visual and contextual sense, from a 10,000-foot view down to the ground view.
- Identify patterns, correlations and causations (including ripple effects) in these layers of metrics that may not be obvious to LoB managers.

- Take all of these individual dashboards and merge them into a rich interactive reporting and inquiry master dashboard.
- Run simulations based on existing metrics to determine the impact that a change in resource allocation (like a 10 percent budget increase or the assignment of more staff) will have on a project timeline.
- Discover synergies between project teams or LoB units that may not yet be collaborating as effectively as they should be.

The value of capturing, connecting and analyzing all of these layers of metrics using cognitive computing and cloud solutions is that decision-makers at every level of the organization can gauge the specific degree to which A causes B and B causes C. (*Data distribution* isn't just about getting data from Point A to Point B. It is also about aggregating and organizing it.) Decision-makers can then run virtualized models along the lines of "If Ax, then Bx, and therefore if Bx, then Cx." (A specific change to A has a high probability of impacting B in a specific way, and therefore the outcome of C as well.) Metrics plus cloud solutions plus cognitive computing equal outcomes that can be more easily optimized.

Remember when we talked about the phase during which a company evolves from *guesstimating* to adopting data-driven decisions? That is what we are talking about here. However, this cannot happen unless every layer of the organization is a) measuring what needs to be measured and b) in the way that it needs to be measured (translation: accurately). Fortunately, cognitive computing can help take some of the guesswork out of the process, so the risk of human error (overlooking a particular metric or measuring it incorrectly) is minimized.

WHEN IN DOUBT, FALL BACK ON THE BASICS.

Let's take a giant step back from this somewhat advanced measurement and analysis model which, fully realized, puts you squarely in Phase 4 (and even Phase 5) of your journey of digital transformation. Augmented by technology or not, measurement always boils down to three simple questions: What, why and how?

1. What should we be measuring?
2. Why should we measure it?
3. How should we measure it?

In the interest of being thorough, this is a good time to add a fourth question to that lot:

4. What are we not measuring that we should be measuring?

An organization's ability to answer that all-too-often-forgotten question on a daily probably is what ultimately separates the Blockbusters of the world from the Netflixes of the world. In our experience, what should really keep CEOs up at night isn't so much what they know or what they don't know, but rather what they've missed completely — what they don't even know they don't know.

Of these four questions, the most important may be the second — why? Why should we measure this? Why is it the most important? This question is most important because it speaks to purpose. It speaks to what outcome you are trying to bring about.

Measurement then, to be effective, must be rooted in purpose. What purpose is that? Take your pick of these or add your own:

- Improve our customers' shopping experience so they will spend 15 percent more per visit.
- Drive an 18 percent QoQ increase in sales for our red socks to reduce surplus inventory.
- Shift 35 percent of our sales to mobile during the next 12 months. Improve employee retention from a 22 month average to a 25 month average.

Your goals, objectives and targets drive measurement. Measurement absent purpose is, more often than not, useless. Purpose drives the why, what and how. With this, we have come full circle in our discussion. What is your purpose? Here are some suggestions:

- Is it to adapt to disruption better and faster than you used to?
- Is it to learn how to shift from survivor mode to disruptor mode?
- Is it to shift from merely playing in the product economy and the service economy to also becoming a force to be reckoned with in the experience economy?
- Is it to jumpstart your company's potential for innovation and disruption?
- Is it to make your IT department more agile?
- Is it to grow from a 5 percent market share to a 35 percent market share during the next five years?

Ask anyone at your company to make a list of what they are trying to accomplish. You will find is a mix of overlapping answers (common goals) and answers unique to them (individual goals). Every single one matters to the whole in some way.

Quick tip: Managers who have trouble determining what metrics should matter to them probably don't understand the purpose of their LoB.

Purpose burns at the heart of every business function, every dollar of every single budget, every campaign, every project, every ad buy, every hire, every software solution you deploy, and lights the way to every business metric we have evoked in this chapter and throughout this book. *Purpose* drives everything, and so purpose also drives digital transformation. Metrics are merely the gauges and needles by which your digital transformation's ability to fulfill its purpose, in all of its minutiae, is measured.

CHAPTER 16:

SUMMARIZING THE JOURNEY AND THE FORMULA FOR DIGITAL TRANSFORMATION

BRINGING EVERYTHING TOGETHER

In the early parts of this book, we focused on the need for companies to push past the paradigms of the product and service economies and expand (or evolve) into the experience economy. Although it may seem like the experience economy is something new, it really isn't. Businesses have created experiences since the first caveman opened a cantina. Creating consistently remarkable experiences has been the hallmark and the secret weapon of pretty much every successful, long-lasting brand in history, from Disney and Cartier to Apple and BMW.

The problem for most businesses is that baking experience design into every customer interaction traditionally has been difficult to scale. Luxury brands managed to pull it off by charging a premium for the added quality of service, which, by virtue of its own exclusivity, limited their customer base to a manageable size. Boutique shops and small businesses also enjoyed the ability to concentrate on building relationships and loyalty among their customer bases thanks to their naturally limited size (and the small size of their employee force as well). For large-scale retailers though, the ability to do this consistently (or at all) remained elusive. Today's digital revolution and massive technological advances, however, have caught up with this pain point to such an extent that what was once the principality of small businesses and luxury brands can scale to be part of any organization's core business.

When we say *can*, we really mean *must*. The opportunities opened by cognitive computing, big data, mobile, social, the internet of things, virtual reality, augmented reality, mixed reality, and so on, aren't exactly a secret, and as more companies begin to take advantage of what these advances can do, customer expectations are adjusting to the realities of the experience economy. Personalized commerce is the norm, rather than the exception. Shopping experiences are increasingly seamless across platforms. Payment systems are fast and frictionless. Mobility is the first point of contact and the main point of sale for most retailers. Marketing is increasingly more predictive and customized, rather than noisy and interruptive. CRM, customer insights, predictive analysis, and behavioral modeling now allow companies to target the right customers with the right messages at the right time to minimize noise and maximize positive drivers to transactions and non-transactional engagement. Companies must either adapt to the new reality of doing business in a digitally-assisted, experience-driven world, or they risk being left behind for good.

STEP 1: ACCEPTING THAT THE WORLD HAS CHANGED

The first step in this journey of adaptation is acknowledging that the tectonic plates of business have shifted and the world of business has changed. Not just a little bit either. It has changed a lot, and it has changed fast.

STEP 2: ACCEPTING THAT CHANGE IS NOTHING MORE THAN A WAKE-UP CALL

The second step is to accept that this disruptive change will require businesses to adapt or die. Yes, we are invoking the notion of business and digital Darwinism, and we make no apologies for it. Adapt or die may have been a tad hyperbolic 10 years ago when the big thing was social media, but this is much bigger than that. This change isn't superficial or limited to channels. It is foundational. It reaches into the core of every business function, every line of business, and strikes at the heart of every customer relationship, regardless of the industry or the vertical. Technology is completely changing the face of commerce, healthcare, transportation, and finance. It is fundamentally changing education, manufacturing, logistics, retail, transportation, hiring, business intelligence, IT, and every process, market and institution around us. So again, adapt or die. There is no third choice.

STEP 3: CHOOSING BETWEEN ADAPTATION AND DISRUPTION

The third step is to acknowledge that adaptation may not be enough. Adapting to keep up with technology is a solid business survival strategy. It is a good defensive game. Run with the pack. Don't get left behind. There is nothing wrong with that. There exists, however, especially during this period of transition and turmoil, an opportunity for companies that are willing to adapt a little faster and a tad more aggressively than others to push ahead of their competitors and take the lead. Incumbent brands that are too slow to adapt may fall behind and find themselves disrupted by smaller, more agile competitors. If you are an incumbent brand, let this be a warning to you. If you are not, let this be a once-in-a-brand lifecycle opportunity to take a giant leap forward and turn disruption to your advantage. You *can* get ahead of disruption, and, as you do, you may find yourself in a position to be the *disruptor* rather than the *disruptee*. As initiative always gives you the advantage, the opportunity is there for the taking. Once you understand the binary cycle of adaptation and disruption, the question becomes which one would you rather focus on for the next 20 to 40 years?

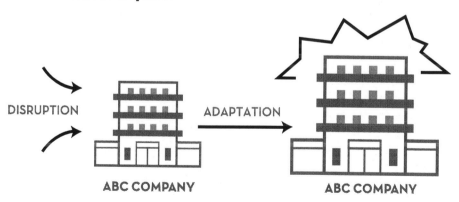

DISRUPTION   ADAPTATION

ABC COMPANY   ABC COMPANY

Fig. 16.1: **Turning Disruption into Opportunity via Adaption**

STEP 4: EYES FORWARD – FROM TODAY TO FIVE YEARS FROM NOW

The fourth step, once you have decided what kind of adaptation you want to pursue (defensive, offensive or a little bit of both), is to think about how technology will help you bridge the gap between where you are and where you could be four or five years from now. Think long (beyond the range of the usual 12-18 month range analysts tend to focus on), but don't get lost in abstract futurism and pipe dreams. Three to give years is ideal for this sort of endeavor. It's important to keep a line of sight on technology's advance in *foreseeable* future. (That's usually four to five years.) The term making the rounds in business strategy circles now is #FYFN (note the hashtag). This stands for *five (or four) years from now*, and typically follows a formulaic *"countdown to"* pattern (2020, 2025, 2030, 2035, and so on). That is the right timeline and the right kind of thinking.

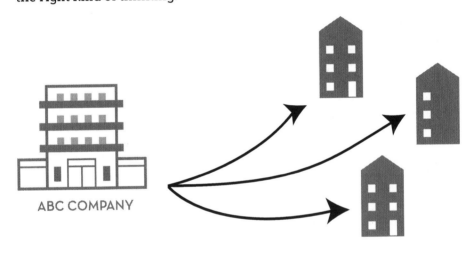

ABC COMPANY

Fig. 16.2: **Disruption as a Model**

STEP 5: LEARNING ABOUT ALL THE NEW TOOLS

Step five involves connecting emerging and developing technologies to specific business (or customer) needs. One aspect of that process focuses on asking general discovery questions like "what can we do with the mobile cloud?" or "what can we do with virtual reality?" This basically is a "tell me what this does and why I should care" phase of technology discovery.

The next logical category of questions focuses on connecting the technology and its general deliverables (better data, faster upload speeds, deeper analytics, lower cost, etc.) to the company's general mission of continuous improvement. What's the macro value of replacing old technology with this new one? What's the value of adopting this new technology?

The third category of questions in this step gets a little more detailed and focuses on specific outcomes. Here, companies typically want to dive a little deeper into their individual lines of business (LOBs) to identify goals, pain points and targets. For instance, a particular sales group might be tasked with growing their sales of intuitive coffee makers by 15 percent YoY. The question would then become *"how can this technology help us grow our sales of intuitive coffee makers by 15 percent YoY?"* (Note that if the group realistically expected to be able to hit an 11 percent target, the question could be rephrased as *"how can this technology help us bridge the gap between 11 percent and 15 percent?"*) If a product group's goal was going from 23 percent to 45 percent market share in the next five years, then the question would be *"how can this technology help us grow our market share from 23 percent to 45 percent in the next five years?"* You get the picture.

The questions don't have to tie back to numbers, by the way. Goals don't have to be targets just yet. For instance, "how can this technology help us understand your customers better?" is a fine question to ask at this juncture. "How can this technology help us drive increasingly rewarding engagements?" is a great one too. Make a list of all of the things you want to do, could do or should do and see how these technologies can help.

Don't forget to consider how some of these technologies might be combined to multiply their effect. For instance, social by itself is great, but social plus big data plus cognitive computing equals much bigger potential for big things.

STEP 6: TRANSITIONING FROM LEARNING TO PLANNING

At this point, you've already given some thought to where the company needs to be four to five years from now, you understand what the new technologies are, and understand exactly how they can help you survive and adapt, fix problems, improve results, and hit specific targets. Now all you need to do is merge that vision and your insights into what technologies you need to adopt, what you will use them for and how you will use them. This is the start of your digital transformation planning. Who will do what? What will go where? How much will this cost? Who will you need to hire? Who will you need to train? How will you structure this evolution? What will the timelines be? What will your KPIs be? What will you prioritize?

STEP 7: TRANSITIONING FROM PLANNING TO BUILDING

Step 7 is pretty simple — less talking, more doing. This is the action phase, when you start putting your plan into action: testing new technologies, adopting them, deploying them, upgrading them, etc. This also is the phase during which your organization begins to change, but we'll get back to that in a minute.

BREAKING DOWN YOUR DIGITAL TRANSFORMATION INTO PHASES.

Let's review the five phases of your digital transformation journey one more time:

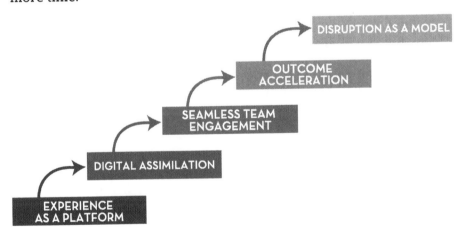

Fig. 16.3: **The 5 Phases of Digital Transformation**

Phase 1: Experience as a platform

The seven steps we just discussed mostly happen in this first phase. The shift to *experience design* that helped drive disruption in your industry is now driving your adaptation. You are in reaction mode and looking for ways to turn experience into a platform. The technology discovery and adoption piece, the digital transformation plan, is the means to that end.

Here, you are setting the stage for your digital transformation. You start to communicate the purpose for your company's digital transformation and your vision for what is to come. This is the phase in which you develop the roadmap for your digital transformation journey, complete with timelines and milestones. You begin to work with every group and department in your company to drive toward this common goal and invite managers to create their own roadmaps and milestones based on their LOBs' needs.

Phase 2: Digital assimilation

You are now beyond just a planning phase. You are testing, doing and building. In this phase, digital thinking becomes part of every aspect of your business. Every digital and tech-related practice that lives on the edges of your business starts becoming part of your *core* business. Mobile, social, experience design, big data, cloud solutions, and cognitive computing all stop being add-ons. In other words, redefine your business in digital terms. Also:

- Embrace mobile as the new primary access point for news, commerce, marketing, and customer experience design ("mobile first").
- Embrace the cloud to reduce costs, make your IT department more agile and accelerate innovation.
- Redefine the role of data in your organization.
- Redefine the role of IT in your organization. (Hybridize it. Operationalize it. Embed IT into every LoB.)

In terms of business practices, not just technology adoption, strive to understand your market and customers better. Find ways to increase the number of *natural* touchpoints with them. Make these touchpoints meaningful and valuable. Build an omnichannel, multiplatform experience ecosystem for your company *around* your customers. Reduce or eliminate friction points between your company and your customers. Empower customers to do business with you where, when and how *they* want. This is the sort of work you can expect to do in this phase.

This is also the phase in which employee engagement and innovation *become* baked into your organization's DNA. This too is a transitional phase. Here are a few quick points of focus to help guide you:

• Develop a culture of continuous improvement in your organization, and turn it into a culture of innovation.
• Build informal innovation centers to encourage initiative, new ideas and purposeful experimentation.
• Build an advanced and frictionless collaboration infrastructure.
• Build a culture of celebration to motivate employees to participate in your transformation

Phase 3: Seamless technology enablement

This is the phase in which new technologies become fully integrated into your business ecosystem. Social, mobile, cloud solutions, SaaS, big data, AI, IoT, automation, and other key technologies are fully coordinated, seamless and easily upgradable. Your IT infrastructure is either hybridized (part legacy/in-house systems and part cloud-based systems) or entirely cloud-based.

This technological transformation phase turns your company into an agile and adaptable business. At this point, technology is no longer a burden. You have learned to use it well, and so it has become a force-multiplier for you.

Phase 4: Outcome acceleration

In this phase, you are increasingly shifting your decision-making toward a data-driven, cognitive computing insights model. (This is where investments in cloud solutions, big data, and AI start paying for themselves.) Your company's continuous improvement model starts to feel effortless. Technological integration is fluid, and both the discovery of new opportunities and your capacity for innovation are part of your core business. Change has become almost frictionless, which means that the speed at which you can analyze, decide, plan, and implement has reached its highest velocity yet.

This is no longer a transition phase. This is an *outcome acceleration* phase. Once you reach it, your company's ability to *adapt, improve* and *innovate* should outpace that of your competitors. It is when you reach this phase that you finally begin to drive market disruption and effectively become a dragon.

Phase 5: Disruption as a model

In this final phase of your transformation, your capacity for market disruption can be multiplied a) by fostering the systematic creation and growth of internal startups, b) by partnering with key vendors, service providers, technology hubs and research labs, and c) through key acquisitions, which generally focus on startups and other technology providers. Disruption is what you do. You are operating entirely as a dragon *and* most likely turning into an accomplished *seeding dragon* as well. Your digital transformation is not over (it never will be), but there is no sixth phase. You have reached your goal. Now all you have to do is keep going.

CHAPTER 17:

WHAT DOES THE FUTURE HOLD FOR DIGITAL TRANSFORMATION AND DISRUPTION?

Throughout this book, we identified how digital transformation, a strategic shift toward the experience economy and a focus on driving innovative disruption can help turn any company into a dragon — a more practical and outcome-driven alternative to the overhyped unicorn. We provided you with a series of practical, adoptable methods for implementing change within your company. We shared the importance of thinking beyond today's business capabilities and how crucial it is for companies, departments and individual professionals to understand where business technology is headed and stay on top of shifting digital trends. Building dragons isn't a rigid process. It's an agile, flexible endeavor. Once you understand its fundamental building blocks, the rest boils down to making the pieces fit however they need to fit for *your* company, *your* organization, and *your* partners and employees.

Dragons all may share similar core traits, but no two dragons are the same. Each dragon is unique. Dragons do share a common wisdom and similar instincts, but they forge their own paths. They borrow, but they never copy. Each one grows, adapts and transforms in its own way. There is only one Amazon, only one Disney and only one Samsung. We can give you the framework, the blueprint, the cheat-sheet, but you have to build your own dragon.

With this in mind, we felt it was appropriate to wrap things up by sharing some market insights on the future of digital transformation.

WHAT THE ANALYSTS PREDICT

Every year large research firms such as Gartner, Forrester and IDC use predictive analysis to gain an understanding of what the future of technology may look like. Most companies are far behind the curve this year. Forrester Research indicates that only 27 percent of operating companies have a working digital strategy, but researchers at Gartner and IDC expect large growth in initiatives and digital revenue during the next four years [37]. Some of the specific predictions that trends and analysis suggest include:

- **Clarifying and unifying the digital vision**. Companies will start to look at the digital big picture, focus on integration, break down departmental silos, and 60 percent of businesses will appoint a new executive to oversee the company's digital vision and drive initiatives forward. [38]

- **The rise of digital revenue streams will change business models**. Until recently, IT departments did not serve direct revenue generating functions. With the creation of more digital revenue, initiatives and challenges, IT departments will play a much larger role within companies of all sizes.

- **Jobs will evolve**. IT professionals will need to expand their reach to new software and devices. As the fields of robotics, AI (artificial intelligence) and IoT (Internet of Things) evolve, many workers will need to develop new skill-sets to manage these technologies.

- **Big data will be more important than ever**. For recognizing shortcomings, new opportunities and streamlining processes, big data will become a staple of business strategy.

- **Connectivity will accelerate digitalization**. The growth of the IoT, in particular, will drive the vision, data usage and evolution of jobs and processes. As more devices connect more people in useful and collaborative ways, every enterprise relationship will change.

---

[37]Press, G. (2015, December 6). Forbes: 6 Predictions About The Future of Digital Transformation. http://www.forbes.com/sites/gilpress/2015/12/06/6-predictions-about-the-future-of-digital-transformation/#78b2ad8c25b4

[38]Press, G. (2015, December 6). Forbes: 6 Predictions About The Future of Digital Transformation. http://www.forbes.com/sites/gilpress/2015/12/06/6-predictions-about-the-future-of-digital-transformation/#78b2ad8c25b4

All of these predictions have one thing in common — change. Companies, departments and individuals need to accept the new reality of constant change to find a place in the digital future.

We all know that many of the challenges that come with a massive organizational change have less to do with identifying the need for change and more to do with the ability to create (and execute) an effective change strategy. Perhaps the most complicated part of digitally transforming a business, especially in the next few years, will be dealing with the velocity of that change. Developing the operational agility to handle the rate and scale of transformation with the new options that make their way to market will be a tremendous challenge, but in this challenge lies a crucial opportunity. Remember what we said about Digital Darwinism. It isn't going to be about survival of the fittest, but about the companies that can learn to be more agile than all of the others. More than ever, the ability to race ahead, anticipate and avoid obstacles along the way, pivot and adapt, then adjust course and race forward again is going to be a key trait of successful companies, particularly dragons. There's no way around it. Companies that don't put change and innovation at the core of their business won't have the tools required to survive.

BE CAUTIOUS OF BLANKET "TRANSFORMATION PLANS"

Authors and strategists often talk about the path of digitalization as though there is a clear blueprint for going digital and disrupting the marketplace. There are some common trends in how successful organizations have adopted digital technologies, but no set of rules can promise digital success.

In fact, it's often what we can't see that will make the most profound impact on the future. Ten years ago, people thought digital media would render newspapers and traditional media obsolete. What they didn't imagine was the fluid connection between print and digital media that many individuals rely on today. Instead of killing or shrinking industries as predicted, digitalization has expanded them and created more opportunities for them than ever before. In spite of the growing pains we have all witnessed in recent years, what we've seen in this evolution, at least for companies and industries that embraced it and adapted to it the fastest, is an expansion of reach, an explosion of capabilities, and the creation of entirely new layers of internal and external connective tissue. These companies and industries may have taken different paths to reach this point, but whether you look at media, healthcare, manufacturing, or business services, these three characteristics have become ubiquitous.

DRIVING INNOVATION WITH VISION

Henry Ford is attributed with saying, "If I had asked people what they wanted, they would have said faster horses." Consumer-centric goals and big data are important, but they will only take digital transformation so far. The truly life-altering changes often come from visionaries who can picture the future and the steps that will bridge the gap between current and future technologies.

Companies need to see what consumers want, but they also need to develop a penchant for recognizing what consumers may not know they yet need. For Ford, the assembly line was only a means to an end — his competitive advantage was his vision for mass-market vehicle manufacturing. The businesses that succeed in the next five to 10 years will recognize the need to change their strategic mindsets, embrace constant change and take calculated risks. One way to think through this problem is simply to ask yourself how a startup might find a way to take market share from you in the next 12-18 months, build that startup yourself, and incorporate its model into your business. That's how you ultimately will learn to shed your own aging skin and stay one step ahead of everyone else. Pretending that change isn't coming, that a brilliant team of tech geniuses isn't secretly plotting to take over your industry right now, is no way to survive the next few decades.

The next piece of the puzzle rests in finding then leveraging whatever combination of new and emerging technologies works best to drive this next evolution faster and better than anyone else might. For your business, digital transformation will be different than for the next company, but the ability to drive innovation in partnership with your customers is what ultimately matters. Henry Ford had to use his instincts to devise the next big idea. The process was mostly just guesswork back then. Today's CEO doesn't have to make those kinds of blind bets. In our era, executives have access to data, intelligent analytics and insights, in real time and at scale. They can leverage powerful product, business and audience modeling tools to discover new opportunities, then figure out how to build entirely new businesses and even verticals around them.

The balance between the unexpected genius of building something entirely new and unexpected for your customers and just giving them what they ask for is still as delicate as ever, but it is nowhere nearly as dangerous or nebulous.

PREPARING FOR A FUTURE OF CHANGE

In the future, we will see an increase in geographical connectedness and mobile device use. Computers will become faster, smaller and more intuitive than ever. Keyboards will cease to be the interface of choice as AI and voice recognition will allow us all to interact with technology through natural speech, as we do with people. Objects around us, from our cars to our children's toys will listen to us, learn from us and strive to improve our lives in ways we are only beginning to understand. We may not be able to clearly see all of the effects that those changes will have on our work and lives yet, but we know these changes are coming and that they will be profound.

Back in 2010 when Blockbuster CEO Jim Keyes was doing that interview with *Fast Company*, it is unlikely he had any idea that, in just a few short years, Blockbuster's reign of the movie rental business in the U.S. would end [39]. Perhaps that is the most interesting thing about disruption and digital transformation. If you ignore it, think you can just wait it out or don't take it seriously enough, your business can be disrupted hard and fast. It doesn't matter how well positioned you *think* you are. If you haven't built an alert, aware, agile, and quickly adaptable organization, you're digital prey. It doesn't matter how big you are or how many years you've been in business. Brand graveyards are filled with incumbent brands that believed their own myths of longevity and invincibility.

In times of change, adaptability equals survival, and adaptability begins with awareness and insight. If you want to survive, you have to see how the world is changing and focus on what is coming. You have to be able to understand it and see the possibilities. Yes, technology may squeeze out old jobs, but it also will create new ones. Yes, technology may weaken some business models, but it also will create entirely new ones. Individuals and companies that understand how to turn a pain point into an opportunity, or leap from an outdated idea to its natural replacement, will not only survive, they will thrive and move up the evolutionary ladder.

Like it or not, technology *will* change the way we learn, the way we get around, the way we play, the way we work, and the way we live. It already is, and there's no stopping it. Companies that get ahead of these changes and help drive them in the most valuable way for specific markets will see their efforts handsomely rewarded, while those that don't will just fall away. Business success in the next few decades will be rooted in a company's ability to transform itself into the type of organization that can drive innovation and disruption. Not all will be dragons, but

[39]Carr, A. (2010, June 08). Blockbuster CEO Jim Keyes on Competition From Apple, Netflix, Nintendo, and Redbox. http://www.fastcompany.com/1656502/blockbuster-ceo-jim-keyes-competition-apple-netflix-nintendo-and-redbox

those that can either *become* dragons or *build* dragons will have an advantage over all others. Just remember that, to drive change on the outside, a company first has to drive change on the inside. One can't happen for any length of time without the other. Change, as a process, as a vehicle for success, has to happen on inside and the outside. Business Darwinism doesn't work any other way.

Bottom line: If you can embrace change instead of fighting it, if you can commit to putting innovation and disruption at the heart of your business model, if you are ready to apply an agile and dynamic startup mentality to your business culture, and if you are willing to work toward *truly* building dragons, the future will be far more packed with possibilities and potential than at any other point in your lifetime.

CHAPTER 18:

BONUS INSIGHTS

During the last few months, we interviewed executives and asked them to share their thoughts on technology, the rise of the experience economy and the role that digital transformation will play in the business world in the coming decades. Here are some of our favorite insights from those conversations:

1. WHAT ARE THE BIGGEST CHALLENGES THAT ORGANIZATIONS FACE WHEN IT COMES TO DIGITAL TRANSFORMATION?

Michael Sutcliff, Group CEO, Accenture Digital:

"There are different challenges depending on the industry, geography, and culture of the company interested in a digital transformation of their business. We believe companies should focus on two different sets of questions to start the conversations on exactly how digital technologies can generate competitive advantage for their specific circumstances.

"The first set of questions relates to the types of experiences they want to deliver to their customers (or patients, students, citizens, employees, etc.). The second set of questions relates to the operating

models they will use to deliver the customer experiences. This combination of customer focused questions and internally focused questions usually allows them to see the entire set of capabilities that will be required to succeed across the journey of their digital transformation.

"Once a company has determined what the future they want to create will look like, they have some work to do in assessing the digital maturity of the industry and geographic footprint of their operations. Matching the introduction of digital solutions to the bandwidths, cost structures, device adoption rates, and content availability in specific markets is an important part of the journey plan.

"The most challenging set of short term constraints many companies face are related to talent. The skills required to take advantage of the digital eco-system as new solutions are designed and built may not be readily available in the existing workforce for a specific company. Many companies find it challenging to understand how to bring together creative design, digital technology, data science, and business model skills in agile teams to support their unique digital transformation needs."

Antonio Lucio, Chief Marketing Officer, HP:

"Mindset. Do you have a digital mindset? If you are not exchanging content and thought leadership with your clients and community you will have a hard time keeping up with your customer community."

Jonathan Becher, Chief Digital Officer, SAP:

"Getting buy-in across the organization. SAP has been phenomenally successful for nearly 45 years. As such, there is a natural resistance to change what has worked so well for so long. In addition, large companies usually have distributed responsibility; decisions and execution require coordination across many stakeholders."

Kevin Bishop, VP, Customer Engagement Solutions, IBM Commerce:

"The greatest challenge CMOs face today is a business challenge - industry convergence. In today's digital world competition often comes from outside traditional spheres of business, with startup

companies challenging well established brands and business models, fuelled by digital innovation. To deal with this, brands need to be willing to embrace creative destruction and reassess their strategic direction as the world around them changes. Leading CMOs, we call them the torchbearers, are re-imagining the way they go to market, experimenting with collaborative business models, creating new offerings and exploiting opportunities for reinvention by integrating marketing, sales and customer service to present a consistent and authentic face to their customers.

"Brands are striving to ensure their services are as seamless as possible for consumers who expect an increasingly personalized and relevant experience across all channels, including mobile and social engagement. To achieve that ideal the best brands put the customer at the center of all decision-making.

"This business challenge then leads to a technical challenge - the challenge of legacy systems, siloed data, and the inability to have a single view of each customer that can be acted on at scale. With the increase in mobile usage, delivering a great experience across all touchpoints is essential. Moving off legacy systems to more adaptable platforms is expressly stated as a core driver towards digital transformation by the torchbearer CMOs cited in the IBM Global C-suite study."

2. HIRING EMPLOYEES WITH DIGITAL DNA (DIGITAL NATIVES) IS BECOMING A MORE POPULAR STRATEGY TO DEAL WITH DIGITAL TRANSFORMATION. HOW DO YOU FIND THIS TYPE OF TALENT AND HOW DO YOU RECOMMEND INCORPORATING THEM INTO THE BUSINESS TO MAXIMIZE ROI?

Michael Sutcliff, Group CEO, Accenture Digital:

"It is absolutely true that technologists, data scientists, designers, and marketing experts who were leading edge practitioners five years ago frequently find themselves working with new toolsets, new eco-system partners, and even new methodologies as they pursue digital transformation initiatives. It is critical to seed the team with a mix of digital native talent who are familiar with the latest tools, techniques, and business partners. The entire team can learn together and move through the learning curve rapidly if there is enough critical mass of digital native talent.

"Finding the talent can be challenging as digital natives frequently have different talent profiles than companies have recruited historically, career tracks which cross multiple disciplines, and fairly specific expectations on work style and culture. We see many clients using our joint engagements to recruit and develop talent in their organizations as they execute the early stages of digital transformation work. We also see clients spending considerable time and money establishing presence in talent markets with attractive digital native populations. Waiting for the traditional recruiting channels and talent markets to provide the digital talent already in high demand does not seem to a reasonable approach for most of our clients."

Antonio Lucio, Chief Marketing Officer, HP:

"Get the Digital Native into big marketing gigs that are properly supported. Make that person visible to the organization. The types of people the CMO hires, develops and promotes send a clear message to the organization as to what is important to the company's transformation."

Kevin Bishop, VP, Customer Engagement Solutions, IBM Commerce:

"Brands now are encouraging a culture where digital is part of everyone's job, just as its part of everyone's life. A strong digital culture is seen as essential to delivering transformational change and is achieved both through experiences that are designed with digital capabilities embedded from the start and through management practices that keep data front and center of every decision. Showcasing internally what is working well in digital also helps to engage people along their digital journey and encourage a cultural change.

"To achieve this, 79 percent of CMOs plan to hire employees with digital skills to improve their marketing function's digital literacy. Most are looking for resources outside their own businesses — three-quarters (74 percent) plan to either partner with other enterprises to tap into their digital expertise or work with consulting firms."

3. HOW DO YOU CONVINCE THE COMPANY LEADERSHIP (OR THE LEADERSHIP OF A KEY LOB) TO AGREE TO SUPPORT INNOVATION OR AN IDEA THAT WILL ULTIMATELY CANNIBALIZE THEIR CASH COW? (THIS IS A QUESTION ABOUT A) LONG TERM VS. SHORT TERM THINKING, AND B) A PLANNED OBSOLESCENCE QUESTION.)

Jonathan Becher, Chief Digital Officer, SAP:

"I think the days are gone that you have to convince a leadership team to support innovation – they all want it but aren't sure how to get there. It's a separate question of whether they would be willing to cannibalize their cash cow. Most want innovation that extends their market reach, rather than replace a current offering. To paraphrase Gordon Moore, legendary CEO of Intel, only the paranoid survive: disrupt yourself before you get disrupted."

4. CAN YOU SHED SOME LIGHT ON HOW PLANNED OBSOLESCENCE (AND PRODUCT LIFE CYCLE PLANNING) CAN HELP ORGANIZATIONS GET BETTER AT ACCELERATING THEIR INNOVATION CYCLES?

Jonathan Becher, Chief Digital Officer, SAP:

"I'd advise looking at the concept of minimal viable product instead. A successful digital culture embraces a minimal viable product with rapid iterations. This goes beyond a first-mover advantage leading to higher market share; digital cultures operate at a higher frequency than more traditional businesses (e.g. weekly product releases, hourly sales forecasts, 10 min response times to customer inquiries)."

5. WHAT OTHER WAY, BESIDES INCORPORATING PLANNED OBSOLESCENCE ONTO THEIR PRODUCT MANAGEMENT MODEL, CAN ORGANIZATIONS GET BETTER AT BECOMING INNOVATION POWERHOUSES?

Jonathan Becher, Chief Digital Officer, SAP:

"There is a big difference between designing things to break or wear out (the traditional definition of planned obsolescence) and designing things to evolve and improve over time. I'd challenge you to reconsider the premise that planned obsolescence is a path to becoming an innovation powerhouse. Instead embrace the concept

of minimal viable product with rapid iterations. And then cultivate the right company culture to get you there – improve risk tolerance, be inclusive of diverse backgrounds, encourage people to be hands-on and not outsource their brains."

6. HOW DOES THE EQUATION CHANGE FOR SMALL AND MEDIUM-SIZED BUSINESSES?

Jonathan Becher, Chief Digital Officer, SAP:

"I have had the opportunity to work for large companies and startups. Smaller companies can move from decisions to execution very quickly. However, they can have trouble remaining focused on the long term. Short term opportunities can distract them – especially if they are cash constrained."

ABOUT THE AUTHORS

DANIEL NEWMAN

Daniel Newman is the Co-CEO of V3B, a leading B2B Digital Marketing Agency, CEO of Broadsuite Media Group and a four-time Amazon Best Selling Author. A leading speaker on Technology, Marketing and Social Business, Daniel is a frequent contributor to Forbes, Entrepreneur and The Huffington Post.

OLIVIER BLANCHARD

Olivier Blanchard is a French-born, American-based Brand Management and Digital Marketing consultant, author of two best-selling books, and an acclaimed keynote speaker. He develops digital strategies, deploys social business capabilities, and aligns corporate programs to business goals.

ACKNOWLEDGEMENTS

We would like to take a moment to thank the many people who directly or indirectly influenced this book through their insights, ideas, and the conversations they shared with us. We know that this topic will continue to be one of the most exciting and greatest challenges for businesses around the globe. Your contributions are not only appreciated, but invaluable to driving business digital transformation forward. So in no particular order, thank you for your support.

Patrick Moorhead, Ursula Ringham, Shelly Kramer, Jeremiah Owyang, Scott Monty, Keith Burtis, Christopher Penn, Josh Bernoff, Shel Holtz, Robert Scoble, Shel Israel, Peter Shankman, Jonathan Becher, Antonio Lucio, Steve Jennings, Augie Ray, Brant Bonin Bough, Brian Solis, Richard Binhammer, Reed Smith, Clay Hebert, Kevin Bishop, Michael Sutcliff, Andrew Eklund, Jean-Paul De Clerck, Aviv Canaani, Kim Brater, Brian Fanzo, David Rose, Janice Person, Esteban Contreras, Gavin Heaton, Joshua Garity, Kristi Colvin, Vincent Brissot, Alan Berkson, Laura McKowen, Kevin Green, and to those that we have forgotten here but could never have done this without!

And of course, none of this would be possible without our families. Our wives, who both happen to be named Lisa, and our children who keep us motivated and humbled at all times.

Made in the USA
Lexington, KY
16 March 2017